# BIG IDEAS
# MATH®
## Modeling Real Life

## Grade 1
### Common Core Edition
### Volume 2

## Ron Larson
## Laurie Boswell

BIG IDEAS
LEARNING®

Erie, Pennsylvania
BigIdeasLearning.com

Big Ideas Learning, LLC
1762 Norcross Road
Erie, PA 16510-3838
USA

For product information and customer support, contact Big Ideas Learning
at 1-877-552-7766 or visit us at BigIdeasLearning.com.

**Cover Image**
Valdis Torms, Brazhnykov Andriy/Shutterstock.com

Printed in the U.S.A.

ISBN 13: 978-1-64208-361-3

2 3 4 5 6 7 8 9 10—22 21 20 19 18

# About the Authors

**Ron Larson**

**Ron Larson, Ph.D.,** is well known as the lead author of a comprehensive program for mathematics that spans school mathematics and college courses. He holds the distinction of Professor Emeritus from Penn State Erie, The Behrend College, where he taught for nearly 40 years. He received his Ph.D. in mathematics from the University of Colorado. Dr. Larson's numerous professional activities keep him actively involved in the mathematics education community and allow him to fully understand the needs of students, teachers, supervisors, and administrators.

*Ron Larson*

**Laurie Boswell**

**Laurie Boswell, Ed.D.,** is the former Head of School at Riverside School in Lyndonville, Vermont. In addition to textbook authoring, she provides mathematics consulting and embedded coaching sessions. Dr. Boswell received her Ed.D. from the University of Vermont in 2010. She is a recipient of the Presidential Award for Excellence in Mathematics Teaching and is a Tandy Technology Scholar. Laurie has taught math to students at all levels, elementary through college. In addition, Laurie has served on the NCTM Board of Directors and as a Regional Director for NCSM. Along with Ron, Laurie has co-authored numerous math programs and has become a popular national speaker.

*Laurie Boswell*

Dr. Ron Larson and Dr. Laurie Boswell began writing together in 1992. Since that time, they have authored over four dozen textbooks. This successful collaboration allows for one voice from Kindergarten through Algebra 2.

# Contributors, Reviewers, and Research

Big Ideas Learning would like to express our gratitude to the mathematics education and instruction experts who served as our advisory panel, contributing specialists, and reviewers during the writing of *Big Ideas Math: Modeling Real Life*. Their input was an invaluable asset during the development of this program.

## Contributing Specialists and Reviewers

- **Sophie Murphy**, Ph.D. Candidate, Melbourne School of Education, Melbourne, Australia
  Learning Targets and Success Criteria Specialist and Visible Learning Reviewer

- **Linda Hall**, Mathematics Educational Consultant, Edmond, OK
  Advisory Panel

- **Michael McDowell**, Ed.D., Superintendent, Ross, CA
  Project-Based Learning Specialist

- **Kelly Byrne**, Math Supervisor and Coordinator of Data Analysis, Downingtown, PA
  Advisory Panel

- **Jean Carwin**, Math Specialist/TOSA, Snohomish, WA
  Advisory Panel

- **Nancy Siddens**, Independent Language Teaching Consultant, Las Cruces, NM
  English Language Learner Specialist

- **Kristen Karbon**, Curriculum and Assessment Coordinator, Troy, MI
  Advisory Panel

- **Kery Obradovich**, K–8 Math/Science Coordinator, Northbrook, IL
  Advisory Panel

- **Jennifer Rollins**, Math Curriculum Content Specialist, Golden, CO
  Advisory Panel

- **Becky Walker**, Ph.D., School Improvement Services Director, Green Bay, WI
  Advisory Panel and Content Reviewer

- **Deborah Donovan**, Mathematics Consultant, Lexington, SC
  Content Reviewer

- **Tom Muchlinski**, Ph.D., Mathematics Consultant, Plymouth, MN
  Content Reviewer and Teaching Edition Contributor

- **Mary Goetz**, Elementary School Teacher, Troy, MI
  Content Reviewer

- **Nanci N. Smith**, Ph.D., International Curriculum and Instruction Consultant, Peoria, AZ
  Teaching Edition Contributor

- **Robyn Seifert-Decker**, Mathematics Consultant, Grand Haven, MI
  Teaching Edition Contributor

- **Bonnie Spence**, Mathematics Education Specialist, Missoula, MT
  Teaching Edition Contributor

- **Suzy Gagnon**, Adjunct Instructor, University of New Hampshire, Portsmouth, NH
  Teaching Edition Contributor

- **Art Johnson**, Ed.D., Professor of Mathematics Education, Warwick, RI
  Teaching Edition Contributor

- **Anthony Smith**, Ph.D., Associate Professor, Associate Dean, University of Washington Bothell, Seattle, WA
  Reading and Writing Reviewer

- **Brianna Raygor**, Music Teacher, Fridley, MN
  Music Reviewer

- **Nicole Dimich Vagle**, Educator, Author, and Consultant, Hopkins, MN
  Assessment Reviewer

- **Janet Graham**, District Math Specialist, Manassas, VA
  Response to Intervention and Differentiated Instruction Reviewer

- **Sharon Huber**, Director of Elementary Mathematics, Chesapeake, VA
  Universal Design for Learning Reviewer

## Student Reviewers

- T.J. Morin
- Alayna Morin
- Ethan Bauer
- Emery Bauer
- Emma Gaeta
- Ryan Gaeta
- Benjamin SanFrotello
- Bailey SanFrotello
- Samantha Grygier
- Robert Grygier IV
- Jacob Grygier
- Jessica Urso
- Ike Patton
- Jake Lobaugh
- Adam Fried
- Caroline Naser
- Charlotte Naser

## Research

Ron Larson and Laurie Boswell used the latest in educational research, along with the body of knowledge collected from expert mathematics instructors, to develop the *Modeling Real Life* series. The pedagogical approach used in this program follows the best practices outlined in the most prominent and widely accepted educational research, including:

- *Visible Learning*
  John Hattie © 2009

- *Visible Learning for Teachers*
  John Hattie © 2012

- *Visible Learning for Mathematics*
  John Hattie © 2017

- *Principles to Actions: Ensuring Mathematical Success for All*
  NCTM © 2014

- *Adding It Up: Helping Children Learn Mathematics*
  National Research Council © 2001

- *Mathematical Mindsets: Unleashing Students' Potential through Creative Math, Inspiring Messages and Innovative Teaching*
  Jo Boaler © 2015

- *What Works in Schools: Translating Research into Action*
  Robert Marzano © 2003

- *Classroom Instruction That Works: Research-Based Strategies for Increasing Student Achievement*
  Marzano, Pickering, and Pollock © 2001

- *Principles and Standards for School Mathematics*
  NCTM © 2000

- *Rigorous PBL by Design: Three Shifts for Developing Confident and Competent Learners*
  Michael McDowell © 2017

- Common Core State Standards for Mathematics
  National Governors Association Center for Best Practices and Council of Chief State School Officers © 2010

- *Universal Design for Learning Guidelines*
  CAST © 2011

- Rigor/Relevance Framework®
  International Center for Leadership in Education

- *Understanding by Design*
  Grant Wiggins and Jay McTighe © 2005

- Achieve, ACT, and The College Board

- *Elementary and Middle School Mathematics: Teaching Developmentally*
  John A. Van de Walle and Karen S. Karp © 2015

- *Evaluating the Quality of Learning: The SOLO Taxonomy*
  John B. Biggs & Kevin F. Collis © 1982

- *Unlocking Formative Assessment: Practical Strategies for Enhancing Students' Learning in the Primary and Intermediate Classroom*
  Shirley Clarke, Helen Timperley, and John Hattie © 2004

- *Formative Assessment in the Secondary Classroom*
  Shirley Clarke © 2005

- *Improving Student Achievement: A Practical Guide to Assessment for Learning*
  Toni Glasson © 2009

# Standards for Mathematical Practice

## Make sense of problems and persevere in solving them.
- Multiple representations are presented to help students move from concrete to representative and into abstract thinking.
- *Think and Grow: Modeling Real Life* examples use problem-solving strategies, such as drawing a picture, circling knowns, and underlining unknowns.

## Reason abstractly and quantitatively.
- Visual problem solving models help students create a coherent representation of the problem.
- *Explore and Grows* allow students to investigate math to understand the reasoning behind the rules.
- Questions ask students to explain their reasoning.

## Construct viable arguments and critique the reasoning of others.
- *Explore and Grows* help students make conjectures and build a logical progression of statements to explore their conjecture.
- Exercises, such as *You Be The Teacher* and *Which One Doesn't Belong?*, provide students the opportunity to critique the reasoning of others.

## Model with mathematics.
- Real-life situations are translated into pictures, diagrams, tables, equations, or graphs to help students analyze relations and to draw conclusions.
- Real-life problems are provided to help students learn to apply the mathematics that they are learning to everyday life.
- Real-life problems incorporate other disciplines to help students see that math is used across content areas.

## Use appropriate tools strategically.
- Students can use a variety of hands-on manipulatives to solve problems throughout the program.
- A variety of tool papers, such as number lines and pattern blocks, are available as students consider how to approach a problem.

## Attend to precision.
- Exercises encourage students to formulate consistent and appropriate reasoning.
- Cooperative learning opportunities support precise communication.

## Look for and make use of structure.
- *Learning Targets* and *Success Criteria* at the start of each chapter and lesson help students understand what they are going to learn.
- *Explore and Grows* provide students the opportunity to see patterns and structure in mathematics.
- Real-life problems help students use the structure of mathematics to break down and solve more difficult problems.

## Look for and express regularity in repeated reasoning.
- Opportunities are provided to help students make generalizations.
- Students are continually encouraged to check for reasonableness in their solutions.

# Achieve the Core

## Meeting Proficiency

As standards shift to prepare students for college and careers, the importance of focus, coherence, and rigor continues to grow.

**FOCUS**      *Big Ideas Math: Modeling Real Life* emphasizes a narrower and deeper curriculum, ensuring students spend their time on the major topics of each grade.

**COHERENCE**      The program was developed around coherent progressions from Kindergarten through eighth grade, guaranteeing students develop and progress their foundational skills through the grades while maintaining a strong focus on the major topics.

**RIGOR**      *Big Ideas Math: Modeling Real Life* uses a balance of procedural fluency, conceptual understanding, and real-life applications. Students develop conceptual understanding in every *Explore and Grow*, continue that development through the lesson while gaining procedural fluency during the *Think and Grow*, and then tie it all together with *Think and Grow: Modeling Real Life*. Every set of practice problems reflects this balance, giving students the rigorous practice they need to be college- and career-ready.

## Major Topics in Grade 1

### Operations and Algebraic Thinking
- Represent and solve problems involving addition and subtraction.
- Understand and apply properties of operations and the relationship between addition and subtraction.
- Add and subtract within 20.
- Work with addition and subtraction equations.

### Number and Operations in Base Ten
- Extending the counting sequence.
- Understand place value.
- Use place value understanding and properties of operations to add and subtract.

### Measurement and Data
- Measure lengths indirectly and by iterating length units.

Use the color-coded Table of Contents to determine where the major topics, supporting topics, and additional topics occur throughout the curriculum.

- ■ Major Topic
- ■ Supporting Topic
- ■ Additional Topic

# 1 Addition and Subtraction Situations

# 2 Fluency and Strategies within 10

■ Major Topic
■ Supporting Topic
■ Additional Topic

# 3 More Addition and Subtraction Situations

Let's learn about more addition and subtraction situations!

# 4 Add Numbers within 20

# 5 Subtract Numbers within 20

# Count and Write Numbers to 120

# Compare Two-Digit Numbers

# 8 Add and Subtract Tens

# 9 Add Two-Digit Numbers

# 10 Measure and Compare Lengths

Let's learn how to measure and compare lengths!

# 11 Represent and Interpret Data

# 12 Tell Time

# 13 Two- and Three-Dimensional Shapes

# 14 Equal Shares

# 8 Add and Subtract Tens

- **How do pinwheels move?**
- **A pinwheel spins 40 times. Then it spins 20 more times. How many times does it spin in all?**

# 8 Vocabulary

Review Words
decade numbers
digits

## Organize It

Use the review words to complete the graphic organizer.

[                    ]

| 1 | 2 | 3 | 4 | 5 | 6 | 7 | 8 | 9 | 10 |
|---|---|---|---|---|---|---|---|---|---|
| 11 | 12 | 13 | 14 | 15 | 16 | 17 | 18 | 19 | 20 |
| 21 | 22 | 23 | 24 | 25 | 26 | 27 | 28 | 29 | 30 |
| 31 | 32 | 33 | 34 | 35 | 36 | 37 | 38 | 39 | 40 |
| 41 | 42 | 43 | 44 | 45 | 46 | 47 | 48 | 49 | 50 |
| 51 | 52 | 53 | 54 | 55 | 56 | 57 | 58 | 59 | 60 |
| 61 | 62 | 63 | 64 | 65 | 66 | 67 | 68 | 69 | 70 |
| 71 | 72 | 73 | 74 | 75 | 76 | 77 | 78 | 79 | 80 |
| 81 | 82 | 83 | 84 | 85 | 86 | 87 | 88 | 89 | 90 |
| 91 | 92 | 93 | 94 | 95 | 96 | 97 | 98 | 99 | 100 |
| 101 | 102 | 103 | 104 | 105 | 106 | 107 | 108 | 109 | 110 |
| 111 | 112 | 113 | 114 | 115 | 116 | 117 | 118 | 119 | 120 |

The [                    ]

of 16 are 1 and 6.

## Define It

What am I?

$13 - 3 = B$     $6 - 4 = M$     $4 + 4 = P$     $12 - 8 = R$

$5 + 1 = O$     $1 + 2 = E$     $3 + 2 = L$     $10 - 3 = U$

$5 + 4 = I$     $9 - 8 = N$

| 6 | 8 | 3 | 1 |  | 1 | 7 | 2 | 10 | 3 | 4 |  | 5 | 9 | 1 | 3 |
|---|---|---|---|---|---|---|---|---|---|---|---|---|---|---|---|
|   |   |   |   |   |   |   |   |   |   |   |   |   |   |   |   |

open
number line

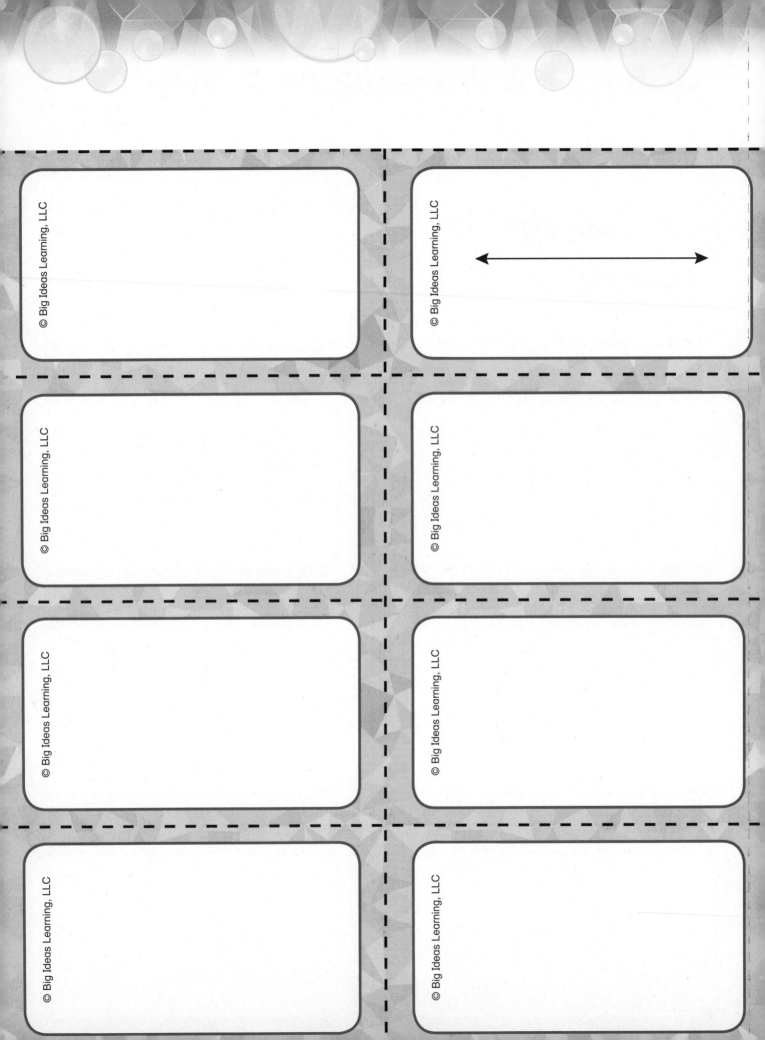

**Learning Target:** Use mental math to add 10.

 Explore and Grow

Find each sum. What do you notice?

$$13 + 10 = \underline{\hspace{1cm}}$$

$$39 + 10 = \underline{\hspace{1cm}}$$

$$52 + 10 = \underline{\hspace{1cm}}$$

$$27 + 10 = \underline{37}$$

| 1 | 2 | 3 | 4 | 5 | 6 | 7 | 8 | 9 | 10 |
|---|---|---|---|---|---|---|---|---|---|
| 11 | 12 | 13 | 14 | 15 | 16 | 17 | 18 | 19 | 20 |
| 21 | 22 | 23 | 24 | 25 | 26 | 27 | 28 | 29 | 30 |
| 31 | 32 | 33 | 34 | 35 | 36 | 37 | 38 | 39 | 40 |
| 41 | 42 | 43 | 44 | 45 | 46 | 47 | 48 | 49 | 50 |
| 51 | 52 | 53 | 54 | 55 | 56 | 57 | 58 | 59 | 60 |
| 61 | 62 | 63 | 64 | 65 | 66 | 67 | 68 | 69 | 70 |
| 71 | 72 | 73 | 74 | 75 | 76 | 77 | 78 | 79 | 80 |
| 81 | 82 | 83 | 84 | 85 | 86 | 87 | 88 | 89 | 90 |
| 91 | 92 | 93 | 94 | 95 | 96 | 97 | 98 | 99 | 100 |

Think of moving down 1 row on a hundred chart.

## Show and Grow

Use mental math.

**1.** $14 + 10 =$ _____

**2.** $46 + 10 =$ _____

**3.** $83 + 10 =$ _____

**4.** $75 + 10 =$ _____

**5.** $21 + 10 =$ _____

**6.** $60 + 10 =$ _____

**7.** $10 + 89 =$ _____

**8.** $10 + 68 =$ _____

Name _____

## ✓ Apply and Grow: Practice

Use mental math.

9.  16 + 10 = _____

10. 63 + 10 = _____

11. 8 + 10 = _____

12. 44 + 10 = _____

13. 19 + 10 = _____

14. 59 + 10 = _____

15. 10 + 22 = _____

16. 10 + 50 = _____

17. 10 + 71 = _____

18. 10 + 38 = _____

19. 55 + _____ = 65

20. 87 + _____ = 97

21. **DIG DEEPER!**  Use each number once to complete
the equations.

    86          76          10          66

    _____ + 10 = _____          _____ + _____ = 96

There are 33 students on a bus. 10 more get on. How many students are on the bus now?

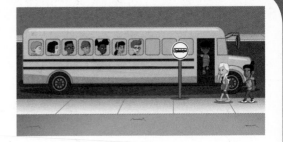

Addition equation:

_____ students

## Show and Grow

22. There are 61 tents at a campground. 10 more are put up. How many tents are at the campground now?

    Addition equation:

_____ tents

Name _____

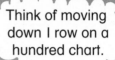

Think of moving down 1 row on a hundred chart.

$$74 + 10 = \underline{84}$$

| 61 | 62 | 63 | 64 | 65 | 66 | 67 | 68 | 69 | 70 |
|----|----|----|----|----|----|----|----|----|-----|
| 71 | 72 | 73 | 74 | 75 | 76 | 77 | 78 | 79 | 80 |
| 81 | 82 | 83 | 84 | 85 | 86 | 87 | 88 | 89 | 90 |
| 91 | 92 | 93 | 94 | 95 | 96 | 97 | 98 | 99 | 100 |

Use mental math.

**1.** $30 + 10 =$ _____

**2.** $81 + 10 =$ _____

**3.** $6 + 10 =$ _____

**4.** $57 + 10 =$ _____

**5.** $48 + 10 =$ _____

**6.** $26 + 10 =$ _____

**7.** $10 + 43 =$ _____

**8.** $10 + 65 =$ _____

**9.** $10 + 82 =$ _____

**10.** $10 + 79 =$ _____

Use mental math.

11. $22 + \underline{\hspace{1cm}} = 32$

12. $85 + \underline{\hspace{1cm}} = 95$

13. $64 + \underline{\hspace{1cm}} = 74$

14. $41 + \underline{\hspace{1cm}} = 51$

15. **DIG DEEPER!** Use each number once to complete the equations.

| | | | |
|---|---|---|---|
| 25 | 10 | 15 | 35 |

$10 + \underline{\hspace{1cm}} = \underline{\hspace{1cm}}$          $25 + \underline{\hspace{1cm}} = \underline{\hspace{1cm}}$

16. **Modeling Real Life** There are 42 teachers at a school. The school hires 10 more. How many teachers are there now?

$\underline{\hspace{1cm}}$ teachers

**Review & Refresh**

17.

10 less than 87 is $\underline{\hspace{1cm}}$.

18.
1 less than 33 is $\underline{\hspace{1cm}}$.

## Explore and Grow

Find each difference. What do you notice?

$$33 - 10 = \underline{\quad}$$

$$67 - 10 = \underline{\quad}$$

$$82 - 10 = \underline{\quad}$$

# Think and Grow

$$36 - 10 = \underline{26}$$

| 1 | 2 | 3 | 4 | 5 | 6 | 7 | 8 | 9 | 10 |
|---|---|---|---|---|---|---|---|---|----|
| 11 | 12 | 13 | 14 | 15 | 16 | 17 | 18 | 19 | 20 |
| 21 | 22 | 23 | 24 | 25 | 26 | 27 | 28 | 29 | 30 |
| 31 | 32 | 33 | 34 | 35 | 36 | 37 | 38 | 39 | 40 |
| 41 | 42 | 43 | 44 | 45 | 46 | 47 | 48 | 49 | 50 |
| 51 | 52 | 53 | 54 | 55 | 56 | 57 | 58 | 59 | 60 |
| 61 | 62 | 63 | 64 | 65 | 66 | 67 | 68 | 69 | 70 |
| 71 | 72 | 73 | 74 | 75 | 76 | 77 | 78 | 79 | 80 |
| 81 | 82 | 83 | 84 | 85 | 86 | 87 | 88 | 89 | 90 |
| 91 | 92 | 93 | 94 | 95 | 96 | 97 | 98 | 99 | 100 |

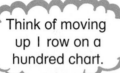

Think of moving up 1 row on a hundred chart.

# Show and Grow

Use mental math.

**1.** $55 - 10 = $ _____

**2.** $21 - 10 = $ _____

**3.** $18 - 10 = $ _____

**4.** $74 - 10 = $ _____

**5.** $89 - 10 = $ _____

**6.** $72 - 10 = $ _____

Name _____

Use mental math.

**7.** $60 - 10 =$ _____

**8.** $45 - 10 =$ _____

**9.** $50 - 10 =$ _____

**10.** $34 - 10 =$ _____

**11.** $51 - 10 =$ _____

**12.** $86 - 10 =$ _____

**13.** $64 - 10 =$ _____

**14.** $97 - 10 =$ _____

**15.** $28 - 10 =$ _____

**16.** $73 - 10 =$ _____

**17.** _____ $- 10 = 22$

**18.** _____ $- 10 = 80$

**19.** **YOU BE THE TEACHER** Is Newton correct? Explain.

$94 - 10 \overset{?}{=} \underline{\textbf{84}}$

_____

_____

_____

You want to ride all 47 rides at an amusement park. You ride 10 of them. How many rides are left?

Subtraction equation:

_____ rides

## Show and Grow

20. You want to try all 65 flavors at a frozen yogurt shop. You try 10 of them. How many flavors are left?

    Subtraction equation:

_____ flavors

**Learning Target:** Use mental math to subtract 10.

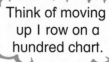

Think of moving up 1 row on a hundred chart.

$$83 - 10 = \underline{73}$$

| 61 | 62 | 63 | 64 | 65 | 66 | 67 | 68 | 69 | 70 |
| 71 | 72 | 73 | 74 | 75 | 76 | 77 | 78 | 79 | 80 |
| 81 | 82 | 83 | 84 | 85 | 86 | 87 | 88 | 89 | 90 |
| 91 | 92 | 93 | 94 | 95 | 96 | 97 | 98 | 99 | 100 |

Use mental math.

**1.** $12 - 10 = \underline{\hphantom{00}}$

**2.** $49 - 10 = \underline{\hphantom{00}}$

**3.** $37 - 10 = \underline{\hphantom{00}}$

**4.** $26 - 10 = \underline{\hphantom{00}}$

**5.** $40 - 10 = \underline{\hphantom{00}}$

**6.** $62 - 10 = \underline{\hphantom{00}}$

**7.** $88 - 10 = \underline{\hphantom{00}}$

**8.** $91 - 10 = \underline{\hphantom{00}}$

**9.** $54 - 10 = \underline{\hphantom{00}}$

**10.** $76 - 10 = \underline{\hphantom{00}}$

Use mental math.

**11.** _____ − 10 = 15

**12.** _____ − 10 = 77

_____

**13.** _____ − 10 = 34

**14.** _____ − 10 = 53

---

**15.** **YOU BE THE TEACHER** Is Descartes correct? Explain.

$40 - 10 \overset{?}{=} \underline{\textbf{50}}$

_____

_____

---

**16.** **Modeling Real Life** There are 99 levels in a video game. You complete 10 of them. How many are left?

_____ levels

**17.** A group of students are at the arcade. 4 of them leave. There are 5 left. How many students were there to start?

_____ students

414    four hundred fourteen

**Learning Target:** Add tens.

Explore and Grow

Model each problem. How are the problems alike? How are they different?

3 + 2 = ___

30 + 20 = ___

Look at the tens digits. $2 + 5 = 7$, so 2 tens + 5 tens = 7 tens.

$$20 + 50 = ?$$

7 tens is 70.

_2_ tens + _5_ tens = _7_ tens

So,    20    +    50    = _70_.

## Show and Grow

1. $40 + 50 = ?$

   _____ tens + _____ tens = _____ tens

   So, $40 + 50 = $ _____.

2. $30 + 30 = ?$

   _____ tens + _____ tens = _____ tens

   So, $30 + 30 = $ _____.

**Apply and Grow: Practice**

**3.** 20 + 40 = ?

_____ tens + _____ tens = _____ tens

So, 20 + 40 = _____.

**4.** 50 + 30 = ?

_____ tens + _____ tens = _____ tens

So, 50 + 30 = _____.

| | |
|---|---|
| **5.** 40 + 10 = _____ | **6.** 70 + 20 = _____ |
| **7.** 30 + 40 = _____ | **8.** 20 + 60 = _____ |
| **9.** _____ + 10 = 40 | **10.** _____ + 60 = 90 |

**11.** **DIG DEEPER!** Which choices match the model?

50                                    20 + 30

2 tens + 3 ones               1 ten + 4 tens

One tray has 20 meatballs. Another tray has the same number of meatballs. How many meatballs are there in all?

Model:

Addition equation:

_____ meatballs

## Show and Grow

12. One box has 40 bags of pretzels. Another box has the same number of bags. How many bags are there in all?

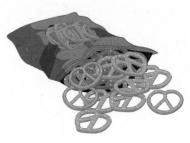

Model:

Addition equation:

_____ bags

**Learning Target:** Add tens.

Look at the tens digits. 6 + 2 = 8, so 6 tens + 2 tens = 8 tens.

8 tens is 80.

$60 + 20 = ?$

__6__ tens + __2__ tens = __8__ tens

So, 60 + 20 = __80__.

**1.** $20 + 70 = ?$

_____ tens + _____ tens = _____ tens

So, 20 + 70 = _____.

**2.** $50 + 30 = ?$

_____ tens + _____ tens = _____ tens

So, 50 + 30 = _____.

**3.** 60 + 20 = _____

**4.** 40 + 40 = _____

**5.** _____ + 40 = 50

**6.** _____ + 30 = 60

**7.** _____ + 20 = 70

**8.** _____ + 50 = 90

**9.** 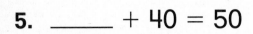 Which choices match the model?

3 tens + 4 ones

5 tens + 2 tens

60

30 + 40

**10.** **Modeling Real Life** One magic set has 30 pieces. Another set has the same number of pieces. How many pieces are there in all?

_____ pieces

**11.** _____ = 6 + 5

**12.** _____ = 3 + 17

**13.** _____ = 11 + 5

**14.** _____ = 5 + 9

**Learning Target:** Use an open number line to add tens.

 **Explore and Grow**

Write the missing numbers. How do the hops help you solve?

$$30 + 20 = \underline{\quad}$$

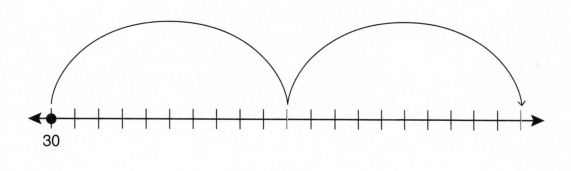

30

## Think and Grow

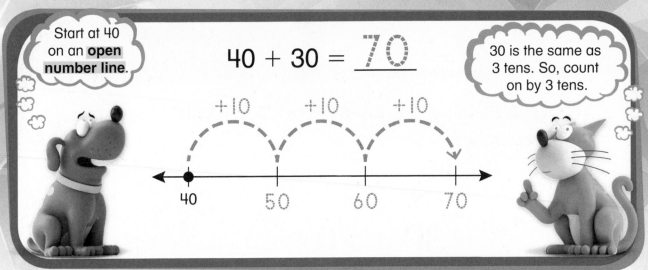

Start at 40 on an **open number line**.

$$40 + 30 = \underline{70}$$

30 is the same as 3 tens. So, count on by 3 tens.

## Show and Grow

1. $50 + 40 = \underline{\phantom{000}}$

50

2. $60 + 20 = \underline{\phantom{000}}$

60

## Apply and Grow: Practice

**3.** 40 + 20 = _____

40

_____

**4.** 50 + 30 = _____ .

_____

**5.** 60 + 40 = _____

_____

**6.** 20 + 50 = _____

_____

**7.**  **Structure** Write an equation that matches the number line.

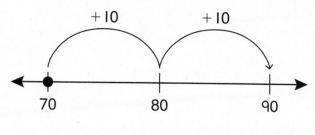

_____ + _____ = _____

You have 20 cans. You collect 20 more cans. Your friend collects 45 cans in all. Who collects more cans?

Model:

⟵————————————————————⟶

Addition equation:

Compare: _____ ◯ _____

Who collects more cans?     You     Friend

## Show and Grow

8. Your class makes 62 paper airplanes. Your friend's class makes 30 small airplanes and 30 large airplanes. Whose class makes more airplanes?

Model:

⟵————————————————————⟶

Addition equation:

Compare: _____ ◯ _____

Whose class makes more airplanes?     Your class     Friend's class

**Learning Target:** Use an open number line to add tens.

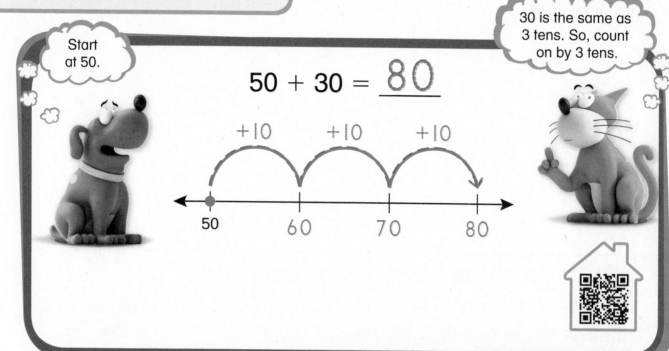

Start at 50.

30 is the same as 3 tens. So, count on by 3 tens.

$$50 + 30 = \underline{80}$$

1. $60 + 30 = \underline{\hspace{1cm}}$

60

2. $20 + 20 = \underline{\hspace{1cm}}$

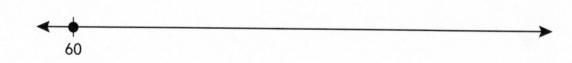

3. $30 + 70 = \underline{\hspace{1cm}}$

**4.**  **Structure** Write an equation that matches the number line.

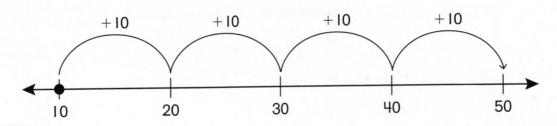

$$\underline{\hspace{1.5em}} + \underline{\hspace{1.5em}} = \underline{\hspace{1.5em}}$$

---

**5. Modeling Real Life** You make 39 snow bricks. Your friend makes 20 small snow bricks and 30 large snow bricks. Who makes more snow bricks?

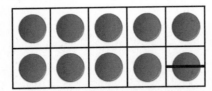

Who makes more snow bricks?    You    Friend

**Review & Refresh**

**6.** Get to 10 to subtract.

$17 - 8 = ?$

$17 - \underline{\hspace{2em}} = 10$

$10 - \underline{\hspace{2em}} = \underline{\hspace{2em}}$

So, $17 - 8 = \underline{\hspace{2em}}$.

**Learning Target:** Subtract tens.

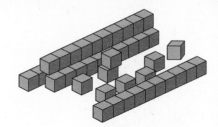

Model each problem. How are the problems alike? How are they different?

$$5 - 2 = \underline{\hspace{1cm}}$$

$$50 - 20 = \underline{\hspace{1cm}}$$

Look at the tens digits.
6 − 4 = 2, so
6 tens − 4 tens = 2 tens.

$$60 - 40 = ?$$

2 tens is 20.

__6__ tens − __4__ tens = __2__ tens

So,     60    −    40    = __20__.

## Show and Grow

1. 70 − 30 = ?

_____ tens − _____ tens = _____ tens

So, 70 − 30 = _____.

2. 40 − 20 = _____

_____ tens − _____ tens = _____ tens

So, 40 − 20 = _____.

## ✓ Apply and Grow: Practice

**3.** $90 - 30 = ?$

_____ tens − _____ tens = _____ tens

So, $90 - 30 =$ _____.

**4.** $50 - 10 = ?$

_____ tens − _____ ten = _____ tens

So, $50 - 10 =$ _____.

**5.** $30 - 20 =$ _____

**6.** $40 - 40 =$ _____

**7.** $80 - 50 =$ _____

**8.** $90 - 70 =$ _____

**9.** $20 -$ _____ $= 10$

**10.** $50 -$ _____ $= 20$

**11.** **DIG DEEPER!** Which choices match the model?

$50 - 30$      $80 - 30$

5 tens − 3 tens      8 tens − 3 tens

You have 80 math problems. You have 40 fewer spelling words. How many spelling words do you have?

```
3+1=4      2+7=4
2+3=5      1+4=5
1+8=9      2+9=11
3+6=9      3+4=7
2+1=3      1+3=4
```

Model:

Subtraction equation:

_____ spelling words

## Show and Grow

**12.** There are 60 students in a play. A football team has 30 fewer students. How many students are on the football team?

Model:

Subtraction equation:

_____ students

**Learning Target:** Subtract tens.

Look at the tens digits.
$9 - 6 = 3$, so
9 tens $-$ 6 tens $=$ 3 tens.

$90 - 60 = ?$

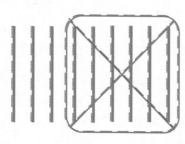

3 tens
is 30.

__9__ tens $-$ __6__ tens $=$ __3__ tens

So,     90     $-$     60     $= \underline{30}$.

**1.** $70 - 50 = ?$

_____ tens $-$ _____ tens $=$ _____ tens

So, $70 - 50 =$ _____.

**2.** $60 - 20 = ?$

_____ tens $-$ _____ tens $=$ _____ tens

So, $60 - 20 =$ _____.

**3.** $60 - 60 =$ _____

**4.** $30 - 10 =$ _____

**5.** 70 − _____ = 0

**6.** 50 − _____ = 40

**7.** 40 − _____ = 20

**8.** 90 − _____ = 50

**9.** **DIG DEEPER!** Which choices match the model?

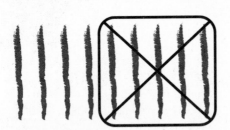

90 − 50          40 − 5

4 tens − 5 ones          9 tens − 5 tens

**10. Modeling Real Life** There are 40 chairs in the library. There are 30 fewer tables than chairs. How many tables are there?

_____ tables

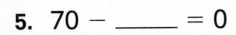
**Review & Refresh**

**11.** 11 − 7 = _____

**12.** 16 − 8 = _____

**13.** 15 − 8 = _____

**14.** 18 − 9 = _____

**Learning Target:** Use an open number line to subtract tens.

**Explore and Grow**

Write the missing numbers. How do the hops help you solve?

$$40 - 20 = \underline{\qquad}$$

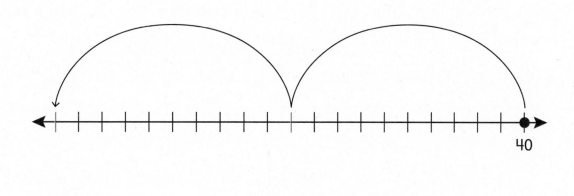

_____          _____

## Think and Grow

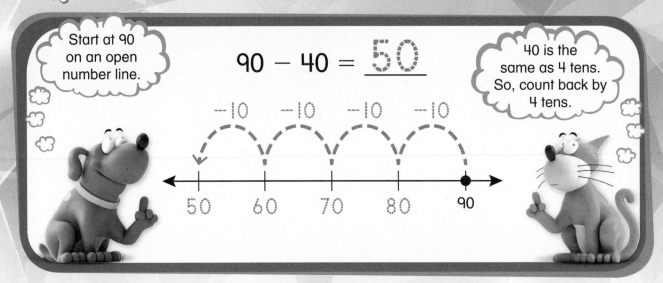

Start at 90 on an open number line.

$90 - 40 =$ **50**

40 is the same as 4 tens. So, count back by 4 tens.

−10  −10  −10  −10

50   60   70   80   90

## Show and Grow

1. $80 - 50 =$ _____

80

2. $70 - 30 =$ _____

70

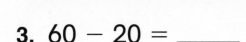 **Apply and Grow: Practice**

**3.** 60 − 20 = _____

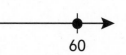

60

**4.** 40 − 30 = _____

**5.** 90 − 40 = _____

**6.** 90 − 70 = _____

**7.** **Structure** Write the equation that matches the number line.

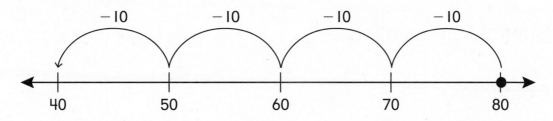

_____ − _____ = _____

© Big Ideas Learning, LLC

You have a bucket of 80 golf balls. You hit 60 of them. Your friend has 28 golf balls left. Who has more golf balls left?

Model:

←————————————————————————→

Subtraction equation:

Compare: _____ ⃝ _____

Who has more golf balls left?     You     Friend

## Show and Grow

8. Pack A has 50 batteries. 40 of them have been used. Pack B has 15 batteries. Which pack has more batteries left?

Model:

←————————————————————————→

Subtraction equation:

Compare: _____ ⃝ _____

Which pack has more batteries left?     Pack A     Pack B

**Learning Target:** Use an open number line to subtract tens.

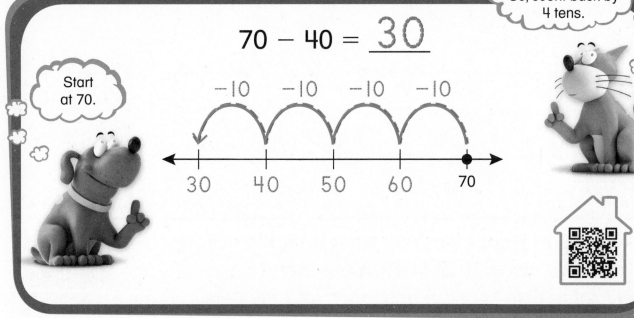

$$70 - 40 = \underline{30}$$

40 is the same as 4 tens. So, count back by 4 tens.

Start at 70.

−10  −10  −10  −10

30   40   50   60   70

**1.** $50 - 30 =$ _____

50

**2.** $80 - 60 =$ _____

**3.** $90 - 20 =$ _____

**4.** 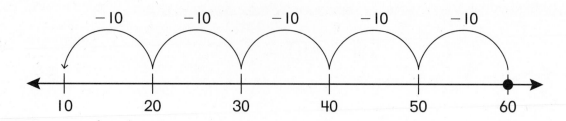 **Structure** Write the equation that matches the number line.

$$\underline{\hspace{1.2cm}} - \underline{\hspace{1.2cm}} = \underline{\hspace{1.2cm}}$$

---

**5. Modeling Real Life** You have 80 raffle tickets and give away 30 of them. Your friend has 47 raffle tickets. Who has more raffle tickets?

Who has more raffle tickets?      You        Friend

**Review & Refresh**

**6.** $13 - 8 = ?$

Think $8 + \underline{\hspace{1cm}} = 13$.

So, $13 - 8 = \underline{\hspace{1cm}}$.

**7.** $15 - 7 = ?$

Think $7 + \underline{\hspace{1cm}} = 15$.

So, $15 - 7 = \underline{\hspace{1cm}}$.

**Learning Target:** Use
addition to subtract tens.

 **Explore and Grow**

## Complete each equation. What do you notice?

20

$$20 + \underline{\quad} = 50$$

50

$$50 - 20 = \underline{\quad}$$

## Think and Grow

**Start at 50.**

$$80 - 50 = ?$$

Count on by tens to get to 80.

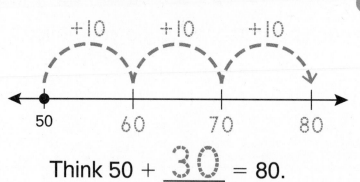

Think 50 + __30__ = 80.

So, 80 − 50 = __30__.

## Show and Grow

**1.** $90 - 70 = ?$

Think 70 + _____ = 90.

So, 90 − 70 = _____.

**2.** $60 - 30 = ?$

Think 30 + _____ = 60.

So, 60 − 30 = _____.

## ✓ Apply and Grow: Practice

**3.** $50 - 30 = ?$

30

Think $30 + $ _____ $= 50$.        So, $50 - 30 = $ _____.

**4.** $70 - 20 = ?$

Think $20 + $ _____ $= 70$.        So, $70 - 20 = $ _____.

**5.** $90 - 50 = ?$

Think $50 + $ _____ $= 90$.        So, $90 - 50 = $ _____.

**6.**  **Structure** Match the related addition and subtraction equations.

$60 + 10 = 70$        $70 - 50 = 20$

$50 + 10 = 60$        $70 - 60 = 10$

$50 + 20 = 70$        $60 - 50 = 10$

A dentist has 40 toothbrushes. She gives away 20 of them. How many toothbrushes does she have left?

Model:

← ————————————————————————————— →

Subtraction equation:

_____ toothbrushes

## Show and Grow

**7.** An art room has 70 bottles of glitter. 30 have been used. How many bottles are left?

Model:

← ————————————————————————————— →

Subtraction equation:

_____ bottles

**Learning Target:** Use addition to subtract tens.

60 − 20 = ?

Start at 20.
Count on by tens
to get to 60.

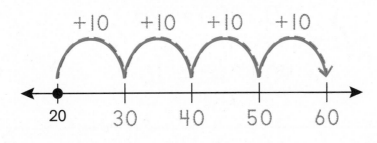

$$\overset{+10}{\frown}\quad\overset{+10}{\frown}\quad\overset{+10}{\frown}\quad\overset{+10}{\frown}$$

20    30    40    50    60

Think 20 + __40__ = 60.

So, 60 − 20 = __40__.

**1.** 70 − 40 = ?

40

Think 40 + _____ = 70.        So, 70 − 40 = _____.

**2.** 90 − 30 = ?

Think 30 + _____ = 90.        So, 90 − 30 = _____.

3. **Structure** Match the related addition and subtraction equations.

$$30 + 10 = 40 \qquad\qquad 50 - 40 = 10$$

$$40 + 10 = 50 \qquad\qquad 50 - 30 = 20$$

$$30 + 20 = 50 \qquad\qquad 40 - 30 = 10$$

4. **Modeling Real Life** Newton has 80 newspapers to deliver. He delivers 50 of them. How many newspapers does he have left?

⟷

_____ newspapers

5. Make quick sketches to compare the numbers.

is greater than

43                          34.

is less than

Add Tens to
a Number

**8.8**

**Learning Target:** Add
tens to a number.

 **Explore and Grow**

Find each sum. What do you notice?

| 1 | 2 | 3 | 4 | 5 | 6 | 7 | 8 | 9 | 10 |
|---|---|---|---|---|---|---|---|---|---|
| 11 | 12 | 13 | 14 | 15 | 16 | 17 | 18 | 19 | 20 |
| 21 | 22 | 23 | 24 | 25 | 26 | 27 | 28 | 29 | 30 |
| 31 | 32 | 33 | 34 | 35 | 36 | 37 | 38 | 39 | 40 |
| 41 | 42 | 43 | 44 | 45 | 46 | 47 | 48 | 49 | 50 |
| 51 | 52 | 53 | 54 | 55 | 56 | 57 | 58 | 59 | 60 |

15 + 10 = _____        27 + 10 = _____

15 + 20 = _____        27 + 20 = _____

15 + 30 = _____        27 + 30 = _____

## Think and Grow

$$16 + 30 = \underline{46}$$

Add the tens. Keep 6 for the ones digit.

**One Way:** Make a quick sketch.

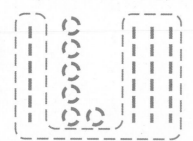

**Another Way:** Use an open number line.

Start at 16. Count on by 3 tens.

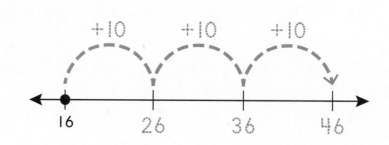

## Show and Grow

**1.** $23 + 50 = \underline{\phantom{00}}$

**2.** $6 + 70 = \underline{\phantom{00}}$

Name _____

**3.** 27 + 40 = _____

**4.** 8 + 80 = _____

**5.** 60 + 35 = _____

**6.** 30 + 44 = _____

**7.** _____ = 33 + 20

**8.** _____ = 70 + 22

---

**9.** **YOU BE THE TEACHER** Is Newton correct? Explain.

36 + 50 $\overset{?}{=}$ **86**

_____

_____

_____

_____

You count 8 birds on your way to school. You count 40 more on your way home. Your friend counts 45 birds in all. Who counts more birds?

Model:

Addition equation:

Compare: _____ ◯ _____

Who counts more birds?     You     Friend

## Show and Grow

**10.** You make 21 snowballs. Your friend makes 11 small snowballs and 20 large snowballs. Who makes more snowballs?

Model:

Addition equation:

Compare: _____ ◯ _____

Who makes more snowballs?     You     Friend

$12 + 20 = \underline{32}$

**One Way:** Make a quick sketch.

Add the tens. Keep 2 for the ones digit.

**Another Way:** Use an open number line.

Start at 12. Count on by 2 tens.

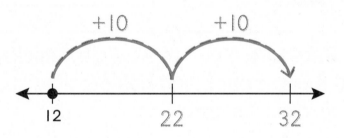

$+10 \qquad +10$

12      22      32

**1.** $19 + 40 = $ _____

**2.** $60 + 23 = $ _____

**3.** _____ = 5 + 90

**4.** _____ = 37 + 30

---

**5.** YOU BE THE TEACHER Is Descartes correct? Explain.

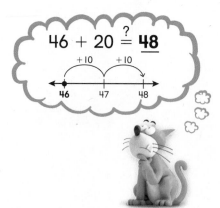

46 + 20 =̇ **48**

+10    +10

46    47    48

_____

_____

_____

_____

---

**6.** **Modeling Real Life** You have 24 glow sticks and buy 40 more. Your friend has 66 glow sticks. Who has more glow sticks?

Who has more glow sticks?    You        Friend

**Review & Refresh**

**7.** Circle the solid shapes that stack.

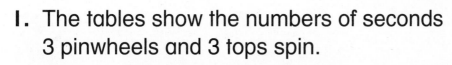

# Performance Task

**8**

**I.** The tables show the numbers of seconds 3 pinwheels and 3 tops spin.

| Pinwheel | Seconds |
|----------|---------|
| Red | 40 |
| Yellow | 90 |
| Blue | |

| Top | Seconds |
|-----|---------|
| Red | |
| Yellow | 50 |
| Blue | 36 |

**a.** How many more seconds does the yellow top spin than the red pinwheel?

_____ seconds

**b.** The red pinwheel spins 30 fewer seconds than the red top. How long does the red top spin?

_____ seconds

**c.** The blue pinwheel and the blue top spin for 96 seconds in all. How long does the blue pinwheel spin?

_____ seconds

**d.** Which pinwheel spins the longest?

Red          Yellow          Blue

# 10 More or 10 Less

**To Play:** Players take turns. On your turn, roll a die to see how many tens you have. Decide whether you want to add 10 to your number or subtract 10 from your number. Place a counter on your sum or difference. Once the board is covered, clear the board and play again.

## **8.1** Mental Math: 10 More

Use mental math.

1. $58 + 10 =$ _____

2. $15 + 10 =$ _____

3. $29 + 10 =$ _____

4. $41 + 10 =$ _____

5. $10 + 7 =$ _____

6. $10 + 36 =$ _____

7. $84 +$ _____ $= 94$

8. $47 +$ _____ $= 57$

## **8.2** Mental Math: 10 Less

Use mental math.

9. $24 - 10 =$ _____

10. $78 - 10 =$ _____

11. $31 - 10 =$ _____

12. $95 - 10 =$ _____

13. _____ $- 10 = 7$

14. _____ $- 10 = 43$

## (8.3) Add Tens

**15.** 60 + 20 = ?

\_\_\_\_\_ tens + \_\_\_\_\_ tens = \_\_\_\_\_ tens

So, 60 + 20 = \_\_\_\_\_.

| | |
|---|---|
| **16.** 30 + 50 = \_\_\_\_\_ | **17.** \_\_\_\_\_ + 30 = 90 |

## (8.4) Add Tens Using a Number Line

**18.** 50 + 40 = \_\_\_\_\_

**19.** (MP) **Structure** Write an equation that matches the number line.

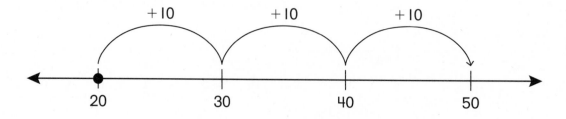

\_\_\_\_\_ + \_\_\_\_\_ = \_\_\_\_\_

## 8.5 Subtract Tens

**20.** 90 − 40 = ?

_____ tens − _____ tens = _____ tens

So, 90 − 40 = _____.

**21.** 70 − 40 = _____

**22.** 80 − _____ = 60

## 8.6 Subtract Tens Using a Number Line

**23.**

60 − 40 = _____

**24.** **MP Structure** Write the equation that matches the number line.

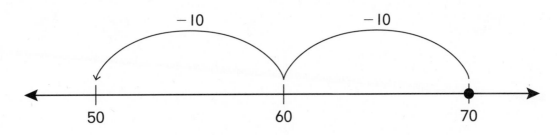

_____ − _____ = _____

## 8.7 Use Addition to Subtract Tens

**25.** $80 - 60 = ?$

60

Think $60 +$ _____ $= 80$.          So, $80 - 60 =$ _____.

**26. Modeling Real Life** A mail carrier has 90 packages to deliver. She delivers 60 of them. How many packages are left?

_____ packages

## 8.8 Add Tens to a Number

**27.** $27 + 50 =$ _____          **28.** _____ $= 80 + 12$

# 9

# Add Two-Digit Numbers

- What are your favorite sports?
- You dribble a basketball 18 times with your right hand and 32 times with your left hand. How many times do you dribble the basketball in all?

# 9 Vocabulary

Review Words
120 chart
column
ones
row
tens

## Organize It

Use the review words to complete the graphic organizer.

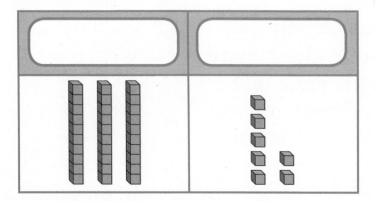

## Define It

Use the review words to complete the puzzle.

### Across

1.

| 1 | 2 | 3 | 4 | 5 | 6 | 7 | 8 | 9 | 10 |
|---|---|---|---|---|---|---|---|---|---|
| 11 | 12 | 13 | 14 | 15 | 16 | 17 | 18 | 19 | 20 |
| 21 | 22 | 23 | 24 | 25 | 26 | 27 | 28 | 29 | 30 |
| 31 | 32 | 33 | 34 | 35 | 36 | 37 | 38 | 39 | 40 |
| 41 | 42 | 43 | 44 | 45 | 46 | 47 | 48 | 49 | 50 |
| 51 | 52 | 53 | 54 | 55 | 56 | 57 | 58 | 59 | 60 |
| 61 | 62 | 63 | 64 | 65 | 66 | 67 | 68 | 69 | 70 |
| 71 | 72 | 73 | 74 | 75 | 76 | 77 | 78 | 79 | 80 |
| 81 | 82 | 83 | 84 | 85 | 86 | 87 | 88 | 89 | 90 |
| 91 | 92 | 93 | 94 | 95 | 96 | 97 | 98 | 99 | 100 |
| 101 | 102 | 103 | 104 | 105 | 106 | 107 | 108 | 109 | 110 |
| 111 | 112 | 113 | 114 | 115 | 116 | 117 | 118 | 119 | 120 |

### Down

2.

| 1 | 2 | 3 | 4 | 5 | 6 |
|---|---|---|---|---|---|
| 11 | 12 | 13 | 14 | 15 | 16 |
| 21 | 22 | 23 | 24 | 25 | 26 |
| 31 | 32 | 33 | 34 | 35 | 36 |

3.

| 1 | 2 | 3 | 4 | 5 |
|---|---|---|---|---|
| 11 | 12 | 13 | 14 | 15 |
| 21 | 22 | 23 | 24 | 25 |
| 31 | 32 | 33 | 34 | 35 |

Name _____

**Learning Target:** Add two numbers by adding the tens and adding the ones.

**Explore and Grow**

Show how you can use a model to solve.

$$32 + 7 = \underline{\quad}$$

| Tens | Ones |
|------|------|
|      |      |

## Think and Grow

$$31 + 14 = \underline{45}$$

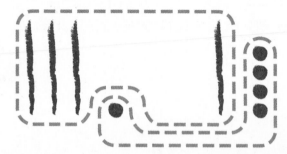

Add the ones. Then add the tens.

## Show and Grow

**1.** $25 + 12 =$ \_\_\_\_

**2.** $36 + 3 =$ \_\_\_\_

**3.** $21 + 8 =$ \_\_\_\_

**4.** $22 + 24 =$ \_\_\_\_

## Apply and Grow: Practice

**5.** 34 + 4 = _____

**6.** 43 + 15 = _____

**7.** 71 + 20 = _____

**8.** 93 + 6 = _____

**9.** 55 + 23 = _____

**10.** 62 + 32 = _____

**11.** **MP Reasoning** Circle the number to complete the equation.

41 + _____ = 46

5              50

## Think and Grow: Modeling Real Life

You watch television for 24 minutes in the morning and 32 minutes at night. How many minutes do you spend watching television in all?

Addition equation:

Model:

_____ minutes

## Show and Grow

12. You do 42 jumping jacks in the morning and 46 at night. How many jumping jacks do you do in all?

Addition equation:

Model:

_____ jumping jacks

$52 + 13 =$ ___65___

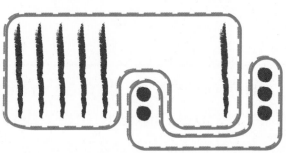

**1.** $42 + 7 =$ _____

**2.** $61 + 35 =$ _____

**3.** $74 + 11 =$ _____

**4.** $86 + 2 =$ _____

**5.** **Reasoning** Circle the number to complete the equation.

$$22 + \underline{\hspace{1cm}} = 92$$

7 70

**6.** **Modeling Real Life** You eat 33 grapes. Your friend eats 23 grapes. How many grapes do you and your friend eat in all?

_____ grapes

**Review & Refresh**

**7.** _____ tens and _____ ones is _____.

**8.** _____ tens and _____ ones is _____.

**Explore and Grow**

Color to show how you can use the hundred
chart to find the sum.

$$23 + 34 = \underline{\hspace{1cm}}$$

| 1 | 2 | 3 | 4 | 5 | 6 | 7 | 8 | 9 | 10 |
|---|---|---|---|---|---|---|---|---|---|
| 11 | 12 | 13 | 14 | 15 | 16 | 17 | 18 | 19 | 20 |
| 21 | 22 | 23 | 24 | 25 | 26 | 27 | 28 | 29 | 30 |
| 31 | 32 | 33 | 34 | 35 | 36 | 37 | 38 | 39 | 40 |
| 41 | 42 | 43 | 44 | 45 | 46 | 47 | 48 | 49 | 50 |
| 51 | 52 | 53 | 54 | 55 | 56 | 57 | 58 | 59 | 60 |
| 61 | 62 | 63 | 64 | 65 | 66 | 67 | 68 | 69 | 70 |
| 71 | 72 | 73 | 74 | 75 | 76 | 77 | 78 | 79 | 80 |
| 81 | 82 | 83 | 84 | 85 | 86 | 87 | 88 | 89 | 90 |
| 91 | 92 | 93 | 94 | 95 | 96 | 97 | 98 | 99 | 100 |

$$26 + 32 = ?$$

**One Way:**

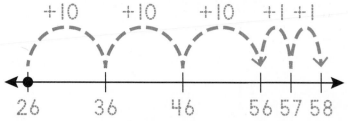

Start at 26. Count by tens, then by ones.

+10  +10  +10  +1 +1

26   36   46   56 57 58

**Another Way:**

You can also count by ones, then by tens.

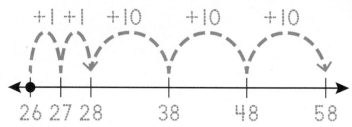

+1 +1  +10  +10  +10

26 27 28   38   48   58

$$26 + 32 = \underline{58}$$

## Show and Grow

1. $22 + 7 =$ _____

22

2. $35 + 41 =$ _____

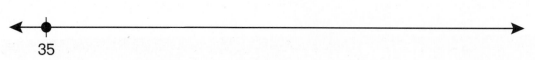

35

## Apply and Grow: Practice

**3.** 53 + 40 = _____

53

**4.** 82 + 12 = _____

**5.** 48 + 31 = _____

**6.** **MP** **Structure** Write an equation that matches the number line.

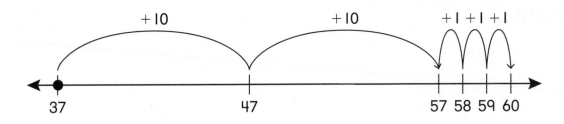

_____ + _____ = _____

The home team scores 37 points. The visiting team scores 22 more. How many points does the visiting team score?

Addition equation:

Model:

← →

_____ points

## Show and Grow

**7.** Your friend scores 63 points. You score 25 more than your friend. How many points do you score?

Addition equation:

Model:

← →

_____ points

**Learning Target:** Use a number line to add two numbers.

Start at 16. Add 1 one, then add 5 tens.

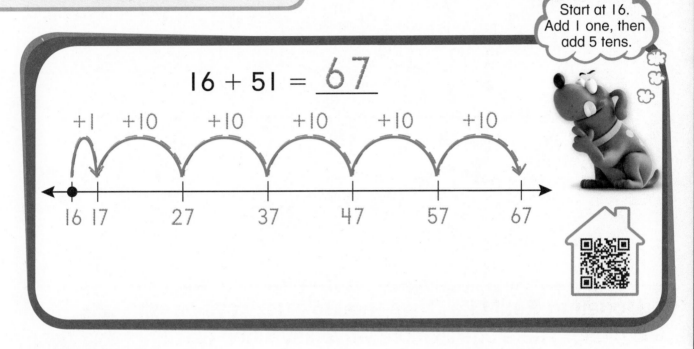

$$16 + 51 = \underline{67}$$

**1.** $13 + 60 = $ _____

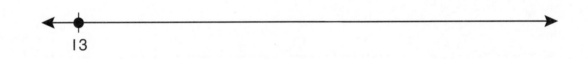

**2.** $81 + 18 = $ _____

**3.** $56 + 42 = $ _____

**4.** 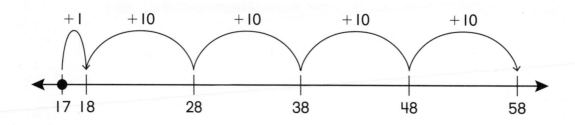 **Structure** Write an equation that matches the number line.

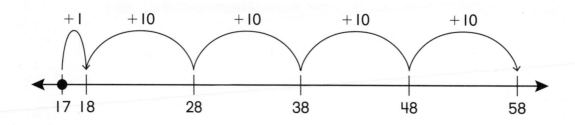

_____ + _____ = _____

---

**5. Modeling Real Life** There are 36 black keys on a piano. There are 16 more white keys than black keys. How many white keys are there?

_____ white keys

**6.** $3 + 7 + 4 =$ _____

**7.** $4 + 5 + 6 =$ _____

**Explore and Grow**

How can you use the model to solve?

$$38 + 6 = \underline{\phantom{000}}$$

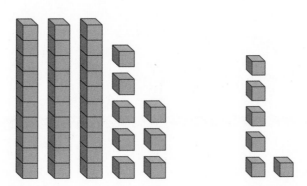

$38 + 5 = \underline{43}$

Make a 10?   (Yes)   No

> When there are 10 or more ones, make a ten.

$38 + 5$

$38 + 2 + 3$

$40 + 3$

$25 + 4 = \underline{29}$

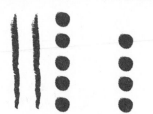

Make a 10?   Yes   (No)

> There are fewer than 10 ones, so you can't make a ten.

## Show and Grow

**1.** $41 + 7 = \underline{\phantom{000}}$

Make a 10?   Yes   No

**2.** $56 + 8 = \underline{\phantom{000}}$

Make a 10?   Yes   No

# ✓ Apply and Grow: Practice

**3.** $72 + 4 =$ _____

Make a 10?   Yes        No

**4.** $63 + 9 =$ _____

Make a 10?   Yes        No

---

**5.** $14 + 6 =$ _____

Make a 10?   Yes        No

**6.** $27 + 5 =$ _____

Make a 10?   Yes        No

---

**7.** $46 + 7 =$ _____

Make a 10?   Yes        No

**8.** $81 + 8 =$ _____

Make a 10?   Yes        No

---

**MP Logic** Complete.

**9.**     $56 + 6$

$56 + \bigcirc + \bigcirc$

$60 + \bigcirc$

$56 + 6 =$ _____

**10.**     $39 + 9$

$39 + \bigcirc + \bigcirc$

$40 + \bigcirc$

$39 + 9 =$ _____

You put 17 puzzle pieces together. There are 7 left. How many puzzle pieces are there in all?

Addition equation:


Model:




Make a 10?     Yes          No


_____ puzzle pieces

## Show and Grow

11. You color 46 states. There are 4 left. How many states are there in all?

    Addition equation:


    Model:

    Make a 10?     Yes          No


_____ states

**Learning Target:** Make a 10 to add a
one-digit number and a two-digit number.

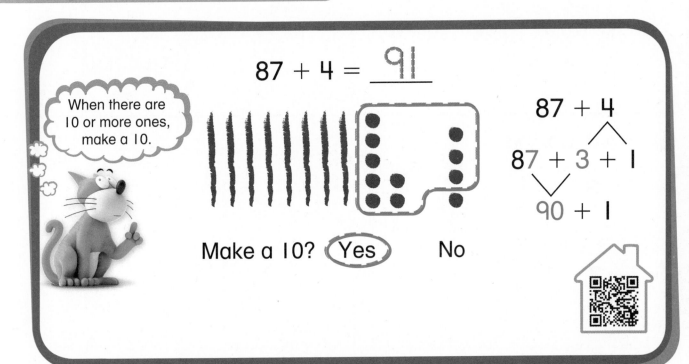

$$87 + 4 = \underline{91}$$

When there are
10 or more ones,
make a 10.

Make a 10? (Yes)    No

$$87 + 4$$
$$87 + 3 + 1$$
$$90 + 1$$

---

**1.** $66 + 5 = $ _____

Make a 10?    Yes    No

**2.** $74 + 3 = $ _____

Make a 10?    Yes    No

---

**3.** $28 + 8 = $ _____

Make a 10?    Yes    No

**4.** $52 + 9 = $ _____

Make a 10?    Yes    No

**5.** 26 + 7 = _____

Make a 10?   Yes          No

**6.** 41 + 6 = _____

Make a 10?   Yes          No

---

 **Logic** Complete.

**7.**

37 + 4

37 + ◯ + ◯

40 + ◯

37 + 4 = _____

**8.**

48 + 6

48 + ◯ + ◯

50 + ◯

48 + 6 = _____

---

**9. Modeling Real Life** A snake lays 24 eggs. Another snake lays 9 eggs. How many eggs are there in all?

_____ eggs

© Big Ideas Learning, LLC

**Review & Refresh**

**10.** Color the shapes that have 4 vertices.

  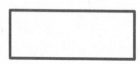 

**Learning Target:** Use place value to add two numbers.

Explore and Grow

Show how you can use a model to solve.

$$43 + 28 = \underline{\quad}$$

| Tens | Ones |
|------|------|
|      |      |
|      |      |
|      |      |
|      |      |
|      |      |

## Think and Grow

Find the number of tens by counting the rods and the group of 10 units.

Find the number of ones by counting the units that are left.

$$26 + 28 = ?$$

| Tens | Ones |
|------|------|
| 26   |      |
| 28   |      |

| | Tens | Ones |
|---|------|------|
|   | 2    | 6    |
| + | 2    | 8    |
|   | 5    | 4    |

_5_ tens _4_ ones

## Show and Grow

1. $39 + 45 = ?$

| | Tens | Ones |
|---|------|------|
| 39 |      |      |
| 45 |      |      |

| | Tens | Ones |
|---|------|------|
|   | 3    | 9    |
| + | 4    | 5    |
|   |      |      |

_____ tens _____ ones

**Apply and Grow: Practice**

**2.** $19 + 35 = ?$

| Tens | Ones |
|------|------|
|      |      |
|      |      |

19

35

| Tens | Ones |
|------|------|
| 1    | 9    |
| + 3  | 5    |
|      |      |

_____ tens _____ ones

**3.**  43
       + 17

| Tens | Ones |
|------|------|
|      |      |
| +    |      |
|      |      |

**4.**  67
       + 14

| Tens | Ones |
|------|------|
|      |      |
| +    |      |
|      |      |

**5.** YOU BE THE TEACHER  Is the sum correct? Explain.

  58
+ 28
——
  76

| Tens | Ones |
|------|------|
| \|\|\|\|\| | • • •  • • •  • • • |
| \|\| | • •  • •  • • |

_____

_____

_____

_____

You earn a sticker for every 10 pages you read. You read 34 pages one week and 37 the next. How many stickers do you earn?

Addition problem:

+ _____
_____

Model:

| Tens | Ones |
|------|------|
|      |      |
|      |      |

Write the missing numbers:

_____ tens _____ one

_____ stickers

## Show and Grow

6. You earn a coin for every 10 cans you recycle. You recycle 18 cans one week and 25 the next. How many coins do you earn?

Addition problem:

+ _____
_____

Model:

| Tens | Ones |
|------|------|
|      |      |
|      |      |

Write the missing numbers:

_____ tens _____ ones

_____ coins

**Learning Target:** Use place value to add two numbers.

16 + 27 = ?

Remember to make a 10 when there are 10 or more ones.

| Tens | Ones |
|------|------|
| 16 | |
| 27 | |

| Tens | Ones |
|------|------|
| 1 | 6 |
| 2 | 7 |
| **4** | **3** |

_4_ tens _3_ ones

1. 57 + 15 = ?

| Tens | Ones |
|------|------|
| 57 | |
| 15 | |

| Tens | Ones |
|------|------|
| 5 | 7 |
| 1 | 5 |
| | |

_____ tens _____ ones

**2.**  $\begin{array}{r} 40 \\ + 36 \\ \hline \end{array}$

| Tens | Ones |
|------|------|
|      |      |
|  +   |      |
|      |      |

**3.**  $\begin{array}{r} 29 \\ + 52 \\ \hline \end{array}$

| Tens | Ones |
|------|------|
|      |      |
|  +   |      |
|      |      |

---

**4.** **DIG DEEPER!** 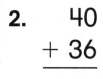 Do you need to use the *make a 10* strategy to find each sum?

$28 + 34 = ?$   Yes   No     $42 + 21 = ?$   Yes   No

$56 + 15 = ?$   Yes   No     $68 + 11 = ?$   Yes   No

---

**5.** You need a box for every 10 muffins you make. You make 33 blueberry muffins and 47 banana muffins. How many boxes do you need?

_____ boxes

**Review & Refresh**

**6.** Is the equation true or false?

$6 + 9 \overset{?}{=} 17 - 1$     $6 + 9:$         $17 - 1:$

_____ $\overset{?}{=}$ _____

True     False

**Learning Target:** Choose a strategy to add two numbers.

**Explore and Grow**

Show two ways you can find the sum.

$$23 + 39 = \underline{\hspace{1cm}}$$

$$23 + 39 = \underline{\hspace{1cm}}$$

$$29 + 36 = ?$$

**One Way:**

$$\begin{array}{r} 29 \\ + 36 \\ \hline 65 \end{array}$$

Choose a strategy.

**Another Way:**

$$29 + 36 = \underline{65}$$

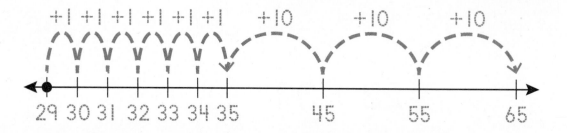

+1 +1 +1 +1 +1 +1 +10 +10 +10

29 30 31 32 33 34 35 45 55 65

## Show and Grow

1. $47 + 24 = $ _____

2. $38 + 43 = $ _____

## ✓ Apply and Grow: Practice

**3.** 22 + 18 = _____

_____

**4.** 57 + 34 = _____

_____

**5.** 73 + 19 = _____

_____

**6.** 81 + 11 = _____

_____

**7.** YOU BE THE TEACHER  Is the sum correct? Explain.

$$17 + 26 \overset{?}{=} \underline{\mathbf{79}}$$

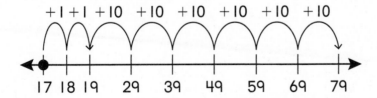

_____

_____

_____

_____

You have 48 songs. Your friend has 27 more than you. How many songs does your friend have?

Addition equation:

Model:

_____ songs

## Show and Grow

8. Your friend sells 56 candles. You sell 35 more than your friend. How many candles do you sell?

Addition equation:

Model:

_____ candles

Name ____________________



**Learning Target:** Choose a strategy to add two numbers.

$34 + 16 = ?$

**One Way:**

$$\begin{array}{r} 34 \\ +\ 16 \\ \hline 50 \end{array}$$

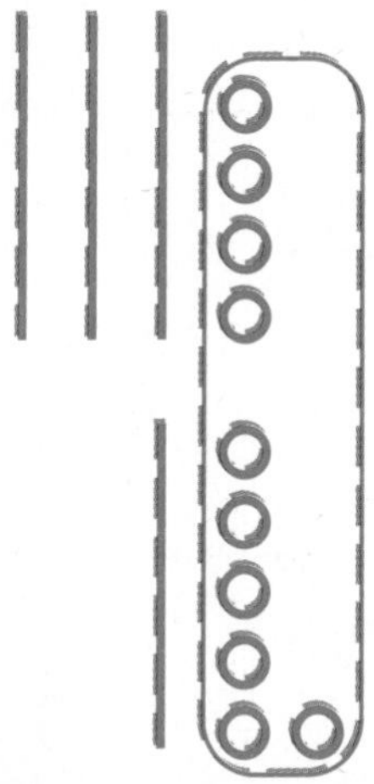

**Another Way:**

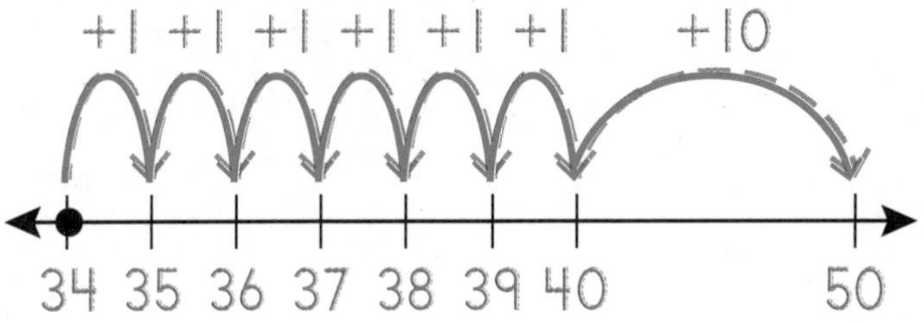
+1 +1 +1 +1 +1 +1 +10
34 35 36 37 38 39 40 50

1. $62 + 29 =$ ______

2. $84 + 8 =$ ______

3. $75 + 17 =$ ______

**4.**  **YOU BE THE TEACHER** Is the sum correct? Explain.

$$\begin{array}{r} 58 \\ + 33 \\ \hline \boxed{91} \end{array}$$

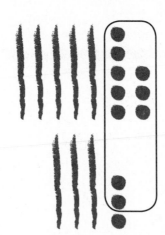

_____

_____

_____

_____

**5. Modeling Real Life** You collect 12 leaves.
Your friend collects 26 more than you.
How many leaves does your friend collect?

_____ leaves

© Big Ideas Learning, LLC

**Review & Refresh**

**6.** Circle the measurable attributes of the table.

length or height        weight        capacity

**Learning Target:** Solve addition word problems.

 **Explore and Grow**

Model the story.

Newton has 15 dog bones. Descartes gives him 8 more. How many dog bones does Newton have now?

_____ dog bones

You ride your bike for 28 minutes. Then you ride your scooter. You ride for 44 minutes in all. How long do you ride your scooter?

Circle what you know.    Underline what you need to find.

Solve:                 $28 + ? = 44$

Use an open number line.

Start at 28. Count on by tens and ones until you reach 44.

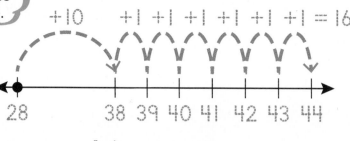

$+10$    $+1$ $+1$ $+1$ $+1$ $+1$ $+1$ $= 16$

28        38 39 40 41 42 43 44

__16__ minutes

## Show and Grow

1. You have 49 toy soldiers. You buy some more. Now you have 84. How many toy soldiers did you buy?

Circle what you know:        Underline what you need to find.

Solve:

_____ toy soldiers

## ✓ Apply and Grow: Practice

**2.** You have 55 pounds of dog food and some cat food. You have 63 pounds of pet food in all. How many pounds of cat food do you have?

Circle what you know.

Underline what you need to find.

Solve:

_____ pounds

---

**3.** A teacher has 34 erasers. There are 46 fewer erasers than pencils. How many pencils are there?

_____ pencils

---

**4.** **DIG DEEPER!** You have 25 toys. Your friend has more than you. There are more than 60 toys in all. How many toys can your friend have?

| 29 | 33 | 24 | 38 |

You need 60 invitations. You have 36 and buy 36 more. Do you have enough invitations?

Circle what you know.

Underline what you need to find.

Solve:

Compare: _____ ◯ 60          Yes          No

## Show and Grow

**5.** You need 84 bottles of water. You have 48 and buy 32 more. Do you have enough bottles of water?

Circle what you know.

Underline what you need to find.

Solve:

Compare: _____ ◯ 84          Yes          No

**Learning Target:** Solve addition word problems.

You have 23 seashells. You find some more. Now you have 39. How many more seashells did you find?

Circle what you know.

Underline what you need to find.

Solve:                23 + ? = 39

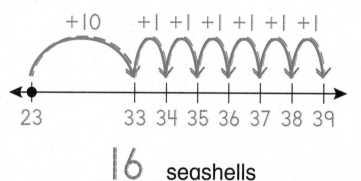

___16___ seashells

**1.** You have 31 stuffed animals. You and your friend have 60 stuffed animals in all. How many stuffed animals does your friend have?

**2.** A store has 56 shirts. There are 28 fewer shirts than pairs of pants. How many pairs of pants are there?

_____ stuffed animals

_____ pairs of pants

**3.** **YOU BE THE TEACHER** You have 25 movies. You have 18 more video games than movies. Your friend says you have 43 movies and video games in all. Is your friend correct? Explain.

_____

_____

**4.** **Modeling Real Life** Newton needs 90 chairs for a party. He has 51. He rents 39 more. Does Newton have enough chairs?

Circle:          Yes          No

Circle the longer object.

**5.**

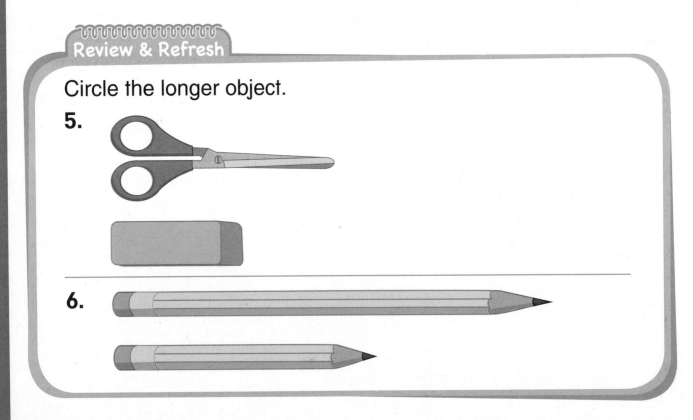

**6.**

**1.** You play a game. Each red ball you collect is worth 10 points. Each yellow ball you collect is worth 1 point.

    **a.** You collect 3 red balls and 13 yellow balls. How many points do you have?

_____ points

**b.** Your teammates score 38 points and 24 points. How many points do your teammates have in all?

_____ points

**c.** Your team wants to have 100 points. Does your team reach its goal?

Yes       No

**d.** Why do you think a red ball is worth more points?

# Race for 100

**To Play:** Take turns. On your turn, roll the dice. Find the sum of the numbers and place that many cubes on your mat. If you have 10 or more cubes in the Ones column, exchange 10 cubes for a rod to place in your Tens column. Continue taking turns until someone reaches 100.

| Tens | Ones |
|------|------|

**9.1** **Add Tens and Ones**

**1.** 56 + 3 = _____

**2.** 22 + 54 = _____

---

**9.2** **Add Tens and Ones Using a Number Line**

**3.** 62 + 25 = _____

---

**4.** 38 + 51 = _____

**5.** **MP** **Structure** Write an equation that matches the number line.

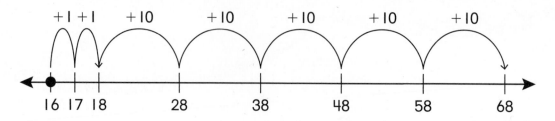

_____ + _____ = _____

---

(**9.3**) **Make a 10 to Add**

**6.** 42 + 6 = _____

Make a 10?   Yes        No

**7.** 27 + 7 = _____

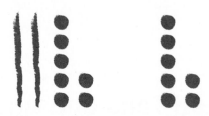

Make a 10?   Yes        No

---

**MP** **Logic** Complete.

**8.**
34 + 7
34 + ◯ + ◯
40 + ◯

34 + 7 = _____

**9.**
59 + 8
59 + ◯ + ◯
60 + ◯

59 + 8 = _____

# 9.4 Add Two-Digit Numbers

Make quick sketches to find the sum.

10. 
$$\begin{array}{r} 28 \\ + 33 \\ \hline \end{array}$$

| Tens | Ones |
|------|------|
|      |      |
|      |      |

_____ tens _____ one

11. 
$$\begin{array}{r} 49 \\ + 24 \\ \hline \end{array}$$

| Tens | Ones |
|------|------|
|      |      |
|      |      |

_____ tens _____ ones

12. **Modeling Real Life** Your club earns a badge for every 10 trees planted. Your club plants 25 trees in the fall and 25 in the spring. How many badges does your club earn?

_____ badges

13. $19 + 43 =$ _____

_____

14. $66 + 28 =$ _____

---

**9.6** **Problem Solving: Addition**

15. Your friend has 59 marbles. You have 23 more than your friend. How many marbles do you have?

_____ marbles

---

16. **Modeling Real Life** You need 50 party hats. You have 24. You buy 16 more. Do you have enough party hats?

Yes          No

# 10

# Measure and Compare Lengths

- Have you ever used a map?
- The red pin shows where you are. Which pin is closest to you? Which pin is farthest from you?

**Chapter Learning Target:**
Understand length.

**Chapter Success Criteria:**
- ▪ I can identify the lengths of objects.
- ▪ I can order objects from longest to shortest.
- ▪ I can compare different lengths.
- ▪ I can measure the length of objects.

# 10 Vocabulary

## Organize It

Use the review words to complete the graphic organizer.

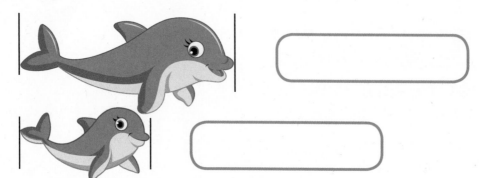

## Define It

Use your vocabulary cards to identify the words. Find each word in the word search.

1.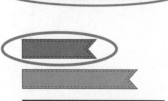

2.

3.

```
K  T  L  M  S  R  A  L  E
G  E  U  B  H  L  Q  O  W
S  R  O  N  O  K  G  N  F
D  C  U  A  R  X  Y  G  I
L  E  N  G  T  H  K  E  V
B  A  N  I  E  W  B  S  O
J  P  U  R  S  O  E  T  Y
C  A  W  S  T  U  N  K  R
L  O  M  E  A  S  U  R  E
```

# Chapter 10 Vocabulary Cards

length

length unit

longest

measure

shortest

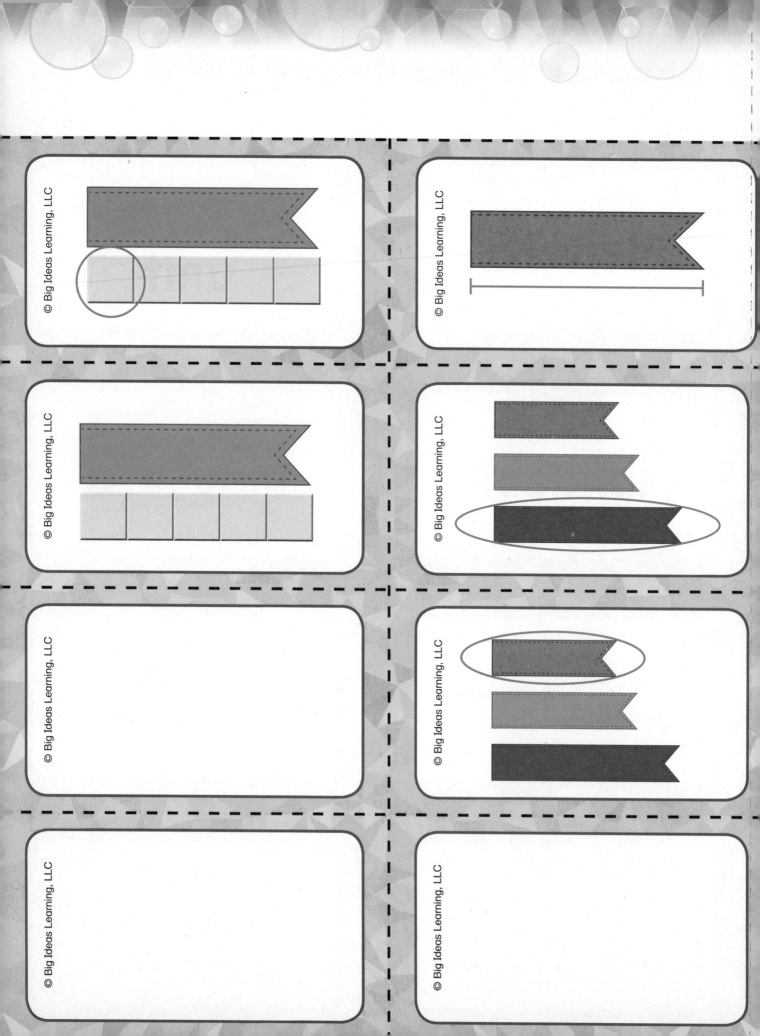

**Learning Target:** Order objects
by length.

 **Explore and Grow**

Draw an object that is shorter than the pencil and
longer than the crayon.

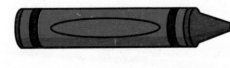

Order from longest to shortest.

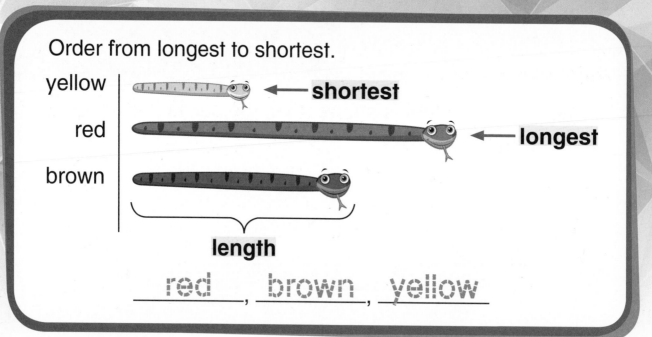

yellow

red

brown

shortest ←

longest ←

length

_____red_____ , ___brown___ , __yellow__

## Show and Grow

**1.** Order from longest to shortest.

purple

blue

pink

_____ , _____ , _____

**2.** Order from shortest to longest.

green

yellow

black

_____ , _____ , _____

**Apply and Grow: Practice**

**3.** Order from longest to shortest.

purple

green

red

_____ , _____ , _____

**4.** Order from shortest to longest.

green

pink

blue

_____ , _____ , _____

**5.** YOU BE THE TEACHER Your friend ordered from shortest to longest. Is your friend correct? Explain.

yellow

red

green

_____

_____

___ yellow ___ , ___ green ___ , ___ red ___

Your yarn is longer than Newton's. Descartes's is longer than Newton's and shorter than yours. Who has the longest yarn?

Draw a picture:

You

Newton

Descartes

Who has the longest yarn?

You          Newton          Descartes

## Show and Grow

**6.** Descartes's pencil is shorter than Newton's. Yours is shorter than Newton's and longer than Descartes's. Who has the shortest pencil?

Draw a picture:

Descartes

Newton

You

Who has the shortest pencil?

Descartes          Newton          You

**Learning Target:** Order objects by length.

Order from longest to shortest.

purple

green

pink

__purple__ , __pink__ , __green__

Order from longest to shortest.

**1.** bat 1

bat 2

bat 3

_____ , _____ , _____

**2.** gold

red

blue

_____ , _____ , _____

**3.** Order from shortest to longest.

vine 1

vine 2

vine 3

———————, ———————, ———————

---

**4.** **DIG DEEPER!** Use the clues to match. The red pencil is longer than the yellow pencil. The shortest pencil is blue.

blue

red

yellow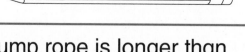

---

**5.** **Modeling Real Life** Your jump rope is longer than Newton's. Descartes's is longer than Newton's and shorter than yours. Who has the longest jump rope?

Who has the longest jump rope?

You     Newton     Descartes

**Review & Refresh**

Compare.

**6.** 25 ◯ 52

**7.** 41 ◯ 44

**Learning Target:** Compare the lengths of two objects using a third object.

**Explore and Grow**

Use string to compare the keys. Which key is longer? How do you know?

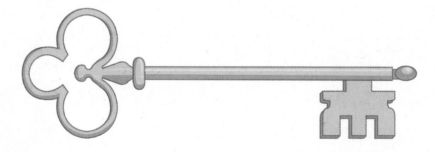

Circle the longer object.

Use the string to compare the lengths.

The stick is longer than the string. The string is longer than the frog. So, the stick is longer than the frog.

## Show and Grow

**1.** Circle the longer object.

**2.** Draw a line through the shorter object.

## ✓ Apply and Grow: Practice

**3.** Draw a line through the shorter object.

_____          _____

---

**4.** Circle the longer object.

_____          _____

---

**5.** **DIG DEEPER!** Which object is longer? Explain.

_____          _____

_____

_____

A green crayon is shorter than a blue crayon. The blue crayon is shorter than a yellow crayon. Is the green crayon longer than or shorter than the yellow crayon?

CRAYONS

Draw a picture:  green

blue

yellow

Longer          Shorter

## Show and Grow

**6.** A yellow ribbon is longer than a pink ribbon. The pink ribbon is longer than a blue ribbon. Is the yellow ribbon longer than or shorter than the blue ribbon?

Draw a picture:  yellow

pink

blue

Longer          Shorter

**Learning Target:** Compare the lengths of two objects using a third object.

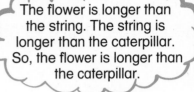

The flower is longer than the string. The string is longer than the caterpillar. So, the flower is longer than the caterpillar.

### Circle the longer object.

**1.** Circle the longer object.

**2.** Draw a line through the shorter object.

3. **DIG DEEPER!** Use the clues to match.

The blue string is longer than the orange string.

The purple string is shorter than the orange string.

blue _____

orange _____

purple _____

---

4. **Modeling Real Life** A kayak is shorter than a canoe. The canoe is shorter than a paddle board. Is the kayak longer than or shorter than the paddle board?

Longer          Shorter

**Review & Refresh**

5. Circle the objects that have capacity as an attribute.

**Learning Target:** Use like objects to measure length.

 Explore and Grow

Find and measure the objects shown in your classroom.

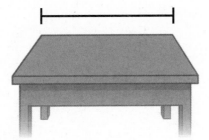

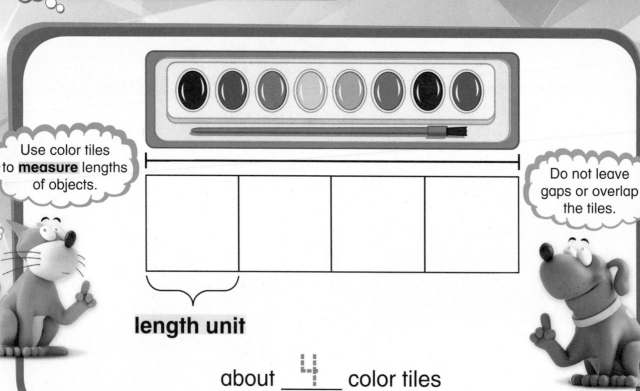

Use color tiles to **measure** lengths of objects.

Do not leave gaps or overlap the tiles.

**length unit**

about ___4___ color tiles

## Show and Grow

Measure.

1.

about _____ color tile

_____

2.

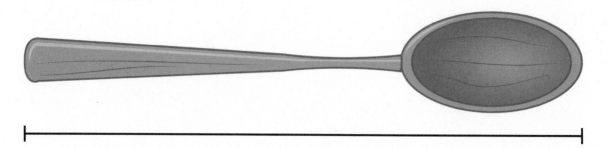

about _____ color tiles

## ✓ Apply and Grow: Practice

Measure.

**3.**

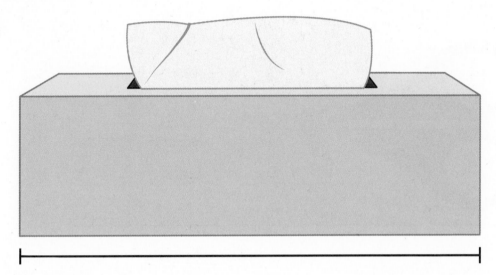

about _____ color tiles

**4.**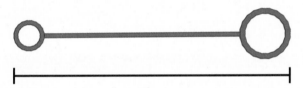

about _____ color tiles

**5.** **MP** **Precision** Which picture shows the correct way to measure the straw?

Will the scissors fit inside a pencil case that is
7 color tiles long?

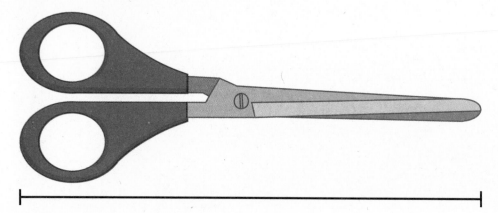

Circle:     Yes          No

Tell how you know:

## Show and Grow

6. Will the cell phone fit inside a case that is
   5 color tiles long?

Circle:     Yes          No

Tell how you know:

Learning Target: Use like objects to measure length.

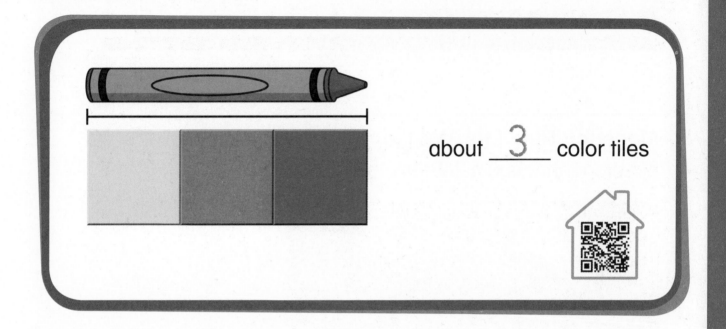

about ___3___ color tiles

Measure.

**1.**

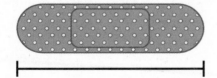

about _____ color tiles

**2.**

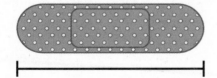

about _____ color tiles

**3.**

about _____ color tiles

**4.** 🔵 **Reasoning** The green yarn is about 3 color tiles long. How long is the blue yarn?

about _____ color tiles

**5. Modeling Real Life** Will the gift card fit inside an envelope that is 8 color tiles long?

GIFT CARD

Circle:  Yes     No

Tell how you know:

**Review & Refresh**

**6.** Complete the fact family.

$7 + 3 =$ _____      _____ $- 3 = 7$

_____ $+$ _____ $=$ _____      _____ $- 7 =$ _____

Learning Target: Measure
an object in different ways.

 Explore and Grow

Find and measure the objects shown in your classroom
two ways. What do you notice?

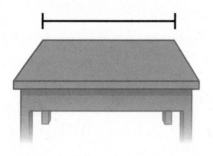

_____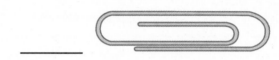

_____

_____

_____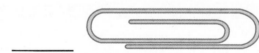

_____

## Think and Grow

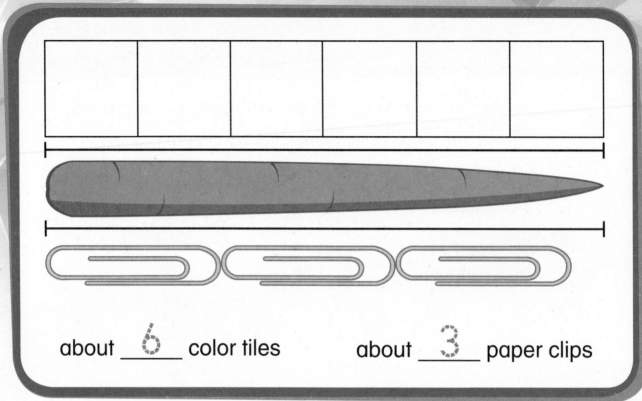

about ___6___ color tiles          about ___3___ paper clips

## Show and Grow

Measure.

**1.**

about _____ color tiles          about _____ paper clips

_____

**2.**

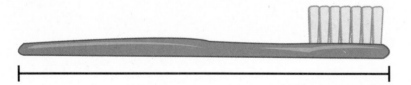

about _____ color tiles          about _____ paper clips

**Apply and Grow: Practice**

Measure.

**3.**

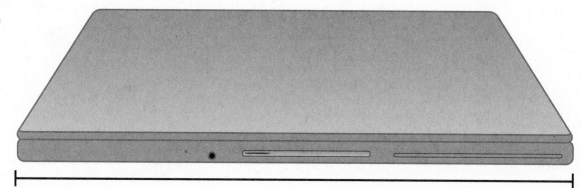

about _____ color tiles          about _____ paper clips

**4.**

about _____ color tiles          about _____ paper clips

**5.** **YOU BE THE TEACHER** Your friend says the pencil is more paper clips long than color tiles. Is your friend correct? Explain.

Your guitar is 33 color tiles long. Is your guitar more than or less than 33 paper clips long?

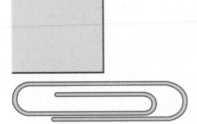

Circle:     more than 33        less than 33

Tell how you know:

## Show and Grow

6. Your mailbox is 11 paper clips long. Is your mailbox more than or less than 11 color tiles long?

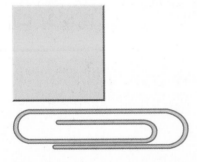

Circle:     more than 11        less than 11

Tell how you know:

**Learning Target:** Measure
an object in different ways.

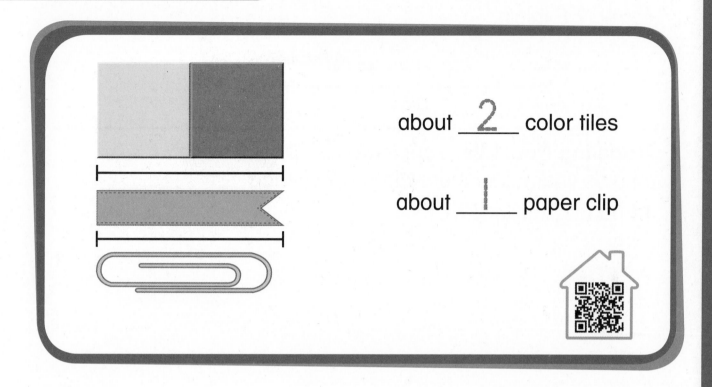

about __2__ color tiles

about __1__ paper clip

Measure.

**1.**

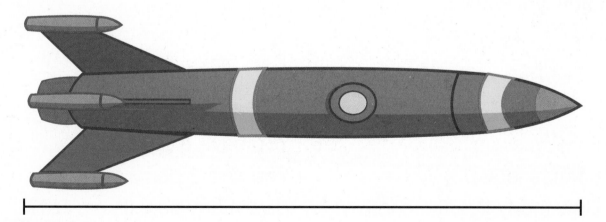

about _____ color tiles          about _____ paper clips

**2.** **YOU BE THE TEACHER** Your friend says the marker is more color tiles long than paper clips. Is your friend correct? Explain.

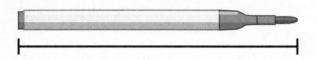

---

**3.** **Modeling Real Life** Your folder is 15 color tiles long. Is your folder more than or less than 15 paper clips long?

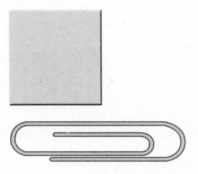

Circle:     more than 15          less than 15

Tell how you know:

**4.** 8 tigers swim.
5 tigers leave.
How many tigers are left?

_____ – _____ = _____

_____ tigers

**5.** You have 6 pencils.
You lose 2 pencils.
How many pencils are left?

_____ – _____ = _____

_____ pencils

**Learning Target:** Solve *compare* word problems involving length.

 **Explore and Grow**

Draw a line that is 2 color tiles longer than the pencil.

Draw a line that is 2 color tiles shorter than the pencil.

Your shoe is 7 color tiles long. Your friend's is 9 color tiles long. How many tiles shorter is your shoe?

Friend: | 9 |

You: | 7 | 2 |

9 -- 7 = 2

7 + 2 = 9

_2_ color tiles

## Show and Grow

1. Your lunch box is 6 paper clips long. Your friend's is 3 paper clips long. How many paper clips longer is your lunch box?

You: | |

Friend: | | |

___ --- ___ = ___

___ + ___ = ___

_____ paper clips

## ✓ Apply and Grow: Practice

**2.** Your scarf is 10 paper clips long. Your friend's is 7 paper clips long. How many paper clips longer is your scarf?

You: ☐

Friend: ☐

_____ − _____ = _____

_____ + _____ = _____

_____ paper clips

---

**3.** Your marker is 6 color tiles long. Your friend's is 7 color tiles long. How many tiles shorter is your marker?

Friend: ☐

You: ☐

_____ ◯ _____ = _____

_____ color tile

---

**4.** 🔵 **Reasoning** Your pencil is 4 color tiles long. Your friend's is 2 color tiles long. Complete the sentences.

Your pencil is _____ color tiles _____ than your friend's.

Your friend's pencil is _____ color tiles _____ than yours.

Your friend's paper chain is 6 paper clips shorter than yours. Your chain is 12 paper clips long. How long is your friend's?

Model:   You:

Friend:

Equation:

_____ paper clips long

## Show and Grow

5. Your paper airplane is 9 color tiles shorter than your friend's. Your friend's paper airplane is 16 color tiles long. How long is yours?

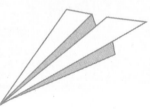

Model:   Friend:

You:

Equation:

_____ color tiles long

**Learning Target:** Solve *compare* word problems involving length.

Your book is 4 color tiles long. Your friend's is 6 color tiles long. How many tiles shorter is your book?

Friend: | 6

You: | 4 | 2

$6 - 4 = 2$

$4 + 2 = 6$

____2____ color tiles

1. Your backpack is 15 paper clips long. Your friend's is 12 paper clips long. How many paper clips longer is your backpack?

You: | 

Friend: | 

____ ___ ___ = ___

____ ___ ___ = ___

_____ paper clips

**2.** **Reasoning** Your baseball mitt is 8 paper clips long. Your friend's is 7 paper clips long. Complete the sentences.

Your friend's baseball mitt is _____ paper clip _____ than yours.

Your baseball mitt is _____ paper clip _____ than your friend's.

**3.** **Modeling Real Life** Your desk is 7 paper clips longer than your friend's. Your friend's desk is 14 paper clips long. How long is yours?

You:

Friend:

_____ paper clips long

**Review & Refresh**

Use the picture to complete the number bond.

**4.**

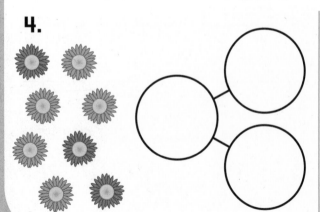

**5.**

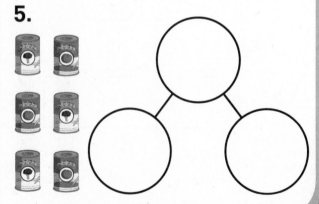

1. Use a piece of string to compare the routes from your house to the library, the post office, and the school. Order the routes from shortest to longest.

_____, _____, _____

2. Use a piece of string to measure the different routes from your house to your friend's house. Color the route you would use to ride your bike to your friend's house.

3. **a.** The bakery is farther from your house than the pool. The park is closer to your house than the pool. Which place is closest to your house?

Park        Bakery        Pool

**b.** Label the park, bakery, and pool on the map.

# Fish Measurement

**To Play:** Flip over 3 Fish Measurement Cards. Compare the lengths of the 3 fish. Place each card in the correct box. Discuss your answers with your partner.

**Shortest**

**Longest**

## 10.1 Order Objects by Length

**1.** Order from longest to shortest.

shark

fish

lobster

_____, _____, _____

**2.** MP **Problem Solving** A green snake is shorter than a black snake. A brown snake is shorter than the black snake. Which snake is the longest?

green          black          brown

## 10.2 Compare Lengths Indirectly

**3.** Circle the longer object.

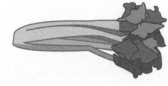

**4.** Circle the longer object.

**5.** Draw a line through the shorter object.

**10.3** **Measure Lengths**

Measure.

**6.**

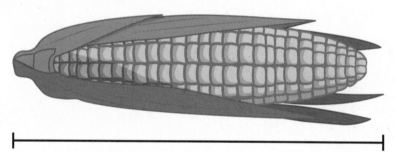

about _____ color tiles

**7.**

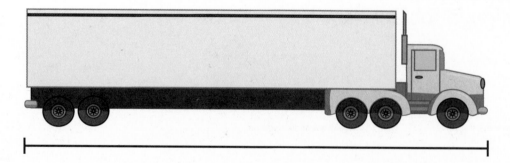

about _____ color tiles

## 10.4 Measure More Lengths

Measure.

**8.**

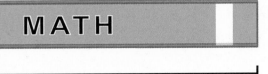

about _____ color tiles          about _____ paper clips

---

**9. Modeling Real Life** Your hockey stick is 18 paper clips long. Is your hockey stick more than or less than 18 color tiles long?

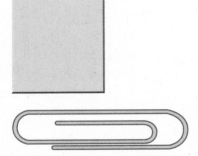

Circle:    more than 18        less than 18

Tell how you know:

## 10.5 Solve *Compare* Problems Involving Length

**10.** Your water bottle is 5 paper clips long. Your friend's is 4 paper clips long. How many paper clips longer is your water bottle?

You:

Friend:

_____ ─── _____ = _____

_____ ─┼─ _____ = _____

_____ paper clip

---

**11.** Your bookshelf is 19 color tiles long. Your friend's is 15 color tiles long. How many tiles longer is your bookshelf?

You:

Friend:

_____ ◯ _____ = _____

_____ color tiles

---

**12.** 🔵 **Reasoning** Your pencil is 6 color tiles long. Your friend's is 3 color tiles long. Complete the sentences.

Your pencil is _____ color tiles _____ than your friend's.

Your friend's pencil is _____ color tiles _____ than yours.

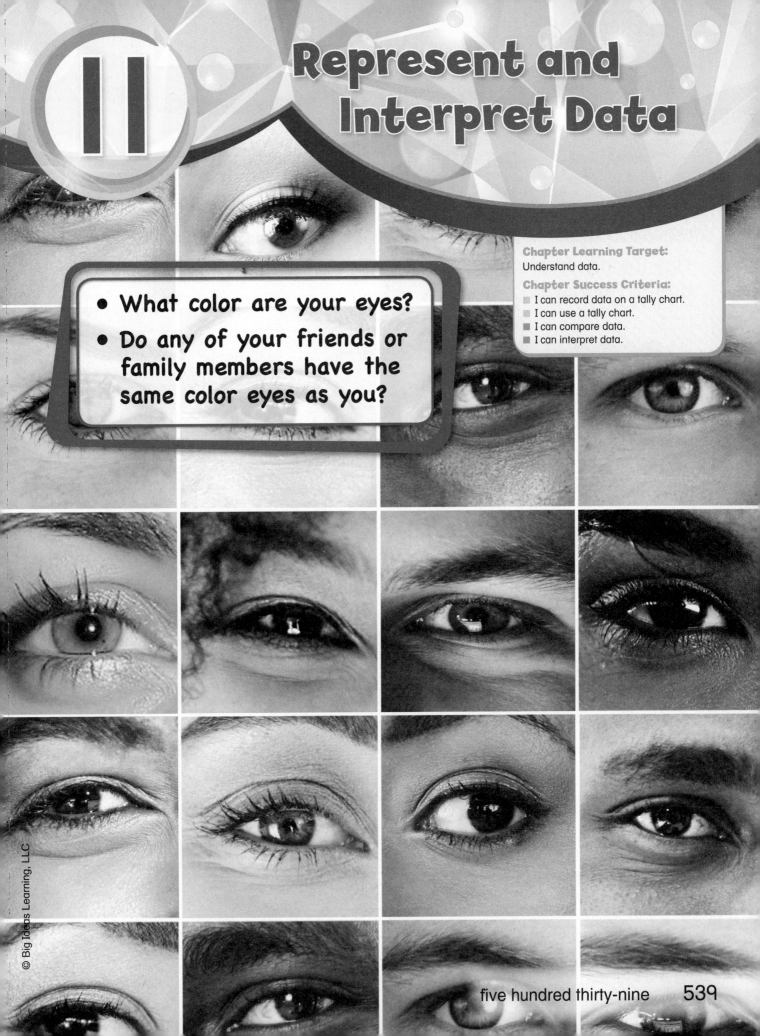

# 11 Represent and Interpret Data

- What color are your eyes?
- Do any of your friends or family members have the same color eyes as you?

**Chapter Learning Target:**
Understand data.

**Chapter Success Criteria:**
- I can record data on a tally chart.
- I can use a tally chart.
- I can compare data.
- I can interpret data.

# 11 Vocabulary

## Organize It

Use the review words to complete the graphic organizer.

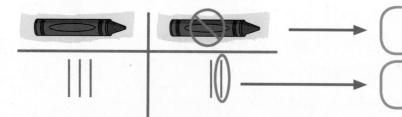

## Define It

Use your vocabulary cards to match.

**1.** bar graph

**Favorite Class**

| ✚ Math | ☺ ☺ ☺ ☺ ☺ ☺ |
|--------|-------------|
| 💡 Science | ☺ ☺ ☺ ☺ ☺ |

Each ☺ = 1 student.

**2.** picture graph

**Favorite Class**

| ✚ Math | ℍℍℍ I |
|--------|-------|
| 💡 Science | ℍℍℍ |

**3.** tally chart

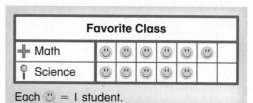

# Chapter 11 Vocabulary Cards

bar graph

data

picture graph

tally chart

tally mark

## Favorite Class

| math | science |
|------|---------|
| science | math |
| science | math |
| math | science |
| math | science |
| math | |

### Favorite Class

| Subject | 0 | 1 | 2 | 3 | 4 | 5 | 6 | 7 |
|---------|---|---|---|---|---|---|---|---|
| ➕ Math | | | | | | | | |
| 🔬 Science | | | | | | | | |

**Number of students**

### Favorite Class

| ➕ Math | 卌 I |
|---------|------|
| 🔬 Science | 卌 |

### Favorite Class

| ➕ Math | 🙂 🙂 🙂 🙂 🙂 🙂 |
|---------|------|
| 🔬 Science | 🙂 🙂 🙂 🙂 🙂 |

Each 🙂 = I student.

### Favorite Class

| ➕ Math | 卌Ⓘ |
|---------|------|
| 🔬 Science | 卌 |

$$I = 1, \text{卌} = 5$$

Name _____

**Learning Target:** Make a tally chart to organize and understand data.

 **Explore and Grow**

Explain how you can sort the objects.

© Big Ideas Learning, LLC

You can organize **data** in a tally chart.

Each **I** means I. Each **IIII** means 5.

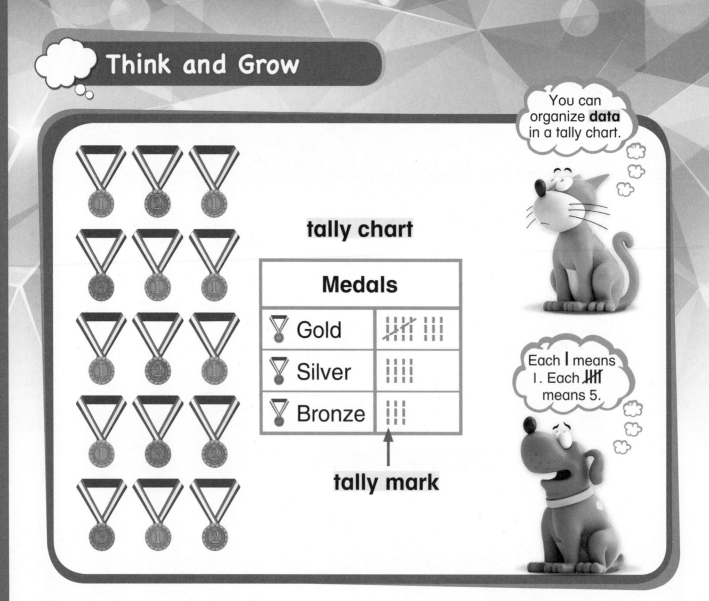

**tally chart**

| Medals | |
|---|---|
| Gold | ~~IIII~~ III |
| Silver | IIII |
| Bronze | III |

**tally mark**

## Show and Grow

1. Complete the tally chart.

| Stickers | |
|---|---|
| Umbrella | |
| Bucket | |
| Crab | |

# ✓ Apply and Grow: Practice

**2.** Complete the tally chart.

| Balls | |
|---|---|
| 🏈 Football | |
| ⚽ Soccer ball | |
| 🏀 Basketball | |

---

**3.** **MP** **Reasoning** Which sentences are correct?

| Stuffed Animals | |
|---|---|
| 🐯 Tiger | ⅢⅢ ⅢⅢ |
| 🦊 Fox | ⅢⅢ ‖ |
| 🦝 Raccoon | ⅢⅢ ‖ |

There are 7 tigers.          The numbers of foxes and raccoons are the same.

There are 7 foxes.          There are 3 raccoons.

## Think and Grow: Modeling Real Life

| Weather | | |
|---|---|---|
| ☀ | Sunny | ЖΉ ||| |
| ☁ | Cloudy | |||| |
| 🌧 | Rainy | ||| |

How many sunny days are there? _____ days

Is the number of cloudy days greater than or less than the number of rainy days?

greater than     less than

## Show and Grow

4.

| Flowers in a Garden | | |
|---|---|---|
| 🌹 | Rose | ЖΉ | |
| 🌻 | Sunflower | || |
| 🌼 | Daisy | ЖΉ || |

How many sunflowers are there? _____ sunflowers

Is the number of roses greater than or less than the number of daisies?

greater than     less than

Name _____

**Learning Target:** Make a tally chart to organize and understand data.

| Ants | |
|---|---|
| Red | ЖЖ IIII |
| Black | ЖЖ I |

**1.** Complete the tally chart.

| Insects | |
|---|---|
| Caterpillar | |
| Fly | |
| Ladybug | |

**2.** **MP** **Reasoning** Which sentences are correct?

| Favorite Movie | |
|---|---|
| Superhero | 卌 |
| Princess | 卌 IIII |
| Mystery | 卌 |

9 students like princess movies.

4 students like superhero movies.

Princess movies are the most favorite.

**3.** **Modeling Real Life** Use the tally chart.

| Favorite Breakfast | |
|---|---|
| Yogurt | 卌 |
| Fruit | IIII |
| Cereal | 卌 I |

How many students chose fruit? _____ students

Is the number of students who chose yogurt greater than or less than the number of students who chose cereal?

greater than       less than

**Review & Refresh**

Compare.

**4.** 45 ◯ 55 | **5.** 74 ◯ 47 | **6.** 22 ◯ 22

Name _____

**Learning Target:** Understand
the data shown by a picture graph.

Read and
Interpret
Picture Graphs

11.2

Explore and Grow

How are the graphs similar? How are they different?

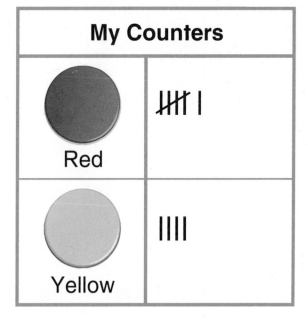

Each ◯ = 1 counter.

# Think and Grow

### picture graph

| Favorite Fruit | | | | | | | | |
|---|---|---|---|---|---|---|---|---|
|  Banana | ☺ | ☺ | ☺ | | | | | |
|  Apple | ☺ | ☺ | ☺ | ☺ | ☺ | ☺ | ☺ | |
|  Orange | ☺ | ☺ | ☺ | ☺ | ☺ | | | |

Each ☺ = I student.

How many students chose banana?  **3**

Which fruit is the most favorite?  🍌  🍎  🍊

## Show and Grow

I.

| Favorite School Trip | | | | | | | | |
|---|---|---|---|---|---|---|---|---|
| Museum | ☺ | ☺ | ☺ | ☺ | ☺ | ☺ | ☺ | ☺ |
| Zoo | ☺ | ☺ | ☺ | ☺ | ☺ | ☺ | | |
| Play | ☺ | ☺ | | | | | | |

Each ☺ = I student.

How many students chose museum? _____

Which trip is the least favorite?

Name _____

2.

| **Favorite Lunch** | | | | | | | | | |
|---|---|---|---|---|---|---|---|---|---|
| Pasta | 🙂 | 🙂 | 🙂 | 🙂 | 🙂 | | | | |
| Soup | 🙂 | 🙂 | 🙂 | | | | | | |
| Taco | 🙂 | 🙂 | 🙂 | 🙂 | 🙂 | 🙂 | 🙂 | 🙂 | |

Each 🙂 = I student.

How many students chose pasta? _____

How many students chose soup? _____

Which lunch is the least favorite?

3. **Writing** In Exercise 2, how do you know which lunch is the most favorite?

_____

_____

_____

### Favorite Activity at the Fair

| | | | | | | | |
|---|---|---|---|---|---|---|---|
| Rides | 🙂 | 🙂 | 🙂 | 🙂 | 🙂 | | |
| Animals | 🙂 | 🙂 | | | | | |
| Games | 🙂 | 🙂 | 🙂 | 🙂 | | | |

Each 🙂 = 1 student.

Is the number of students who chose rides greater than, less than, or equal to the number of students who chose animals?

greater than     less than     equal to

## Show and Grow

**4.**

### Favorite Forest Animal

| | | | | | | | |
|---|---|---|---|---|---|---|---|
| Frog | 🙂 | 🙂 | 🙂 | | | | |
| Bear | 🙂 | 🙂 | 🙂 | 🙂 | 🙂 | 🙂 | |
| Fox | 🙂 | 🙂 | 🙂 | | | | |

Each 🙂 = 1 student.

Is the number of students who chose frog greater than, less than, or equal to the number of students who chose bear?

greater than     less than     equal to

**Learning Target:** Understand the data shown by a picture graph.

| **Favorite Snack** | | | | | | | |
|---|---|---|---|---|---|---|---|
|  Pretzels | 😊 | 😊 | 😊 | 😊 | 😊 | 😊 | |
| 🍎 Apple | 😊 | 😊 | 😊 | | | | |

Each 😊 = 1 student.

Which snack is the most favorite?

1.

| **Favorite Season** | | | | | | | | | |
|---|---|---|---|---|---|---|---|---|---|
| 🌼 Spring | 😊 | 😊 | 😊 | | | | | | |
| ☀️ Summer | 😊 | 😊 | 😊 | 😊 | 😊 | 😊 | 😊 | | |
| 🍂 Fall | 😊 | 😊 | 😊 | 😊 | | | | | |
| ❄️ Winter | 😊 | | | | | | | | |

Each 😊 = 1 student.

How many students chose summer? _____

How many students chose fall? _____

Which season is the least favorite?

**2. Writing** How do you know which category has the least when looking at a picture graph?

_____

_____

_____

_____

**3. Modeling Real Life** Use the picture graph.

| **Favorite Drink at Lunch** | | | | | | | | | |
|---|---|---|---|---|---|---|---|---|---|
| Milk | ☺ | ☺ | ☺ | | | | | | |
| Water | ☺ | ☺ | ☺ | ☺ | | | | | |
| Juice | ☺ | ☺ | ☺ | ☺ | | | | | |

Each ☺ = 1 student.

Is the number of students who chose water greater than, less than, or equal to the number of students who chose juice?

greater than     less than     equal to

**Review & Refresh**

**4.** $31 + 40 = $ _____

**5.** $62 + 20 = $ _____

**Learning Target:** Understand the data shown by a bar graph.

**Explore and Grow**

How are the graphs similar? How are they different?

**Favorite Fruit**

| | Blueberries | 🙂 | 🙂 | 🙂 | | |
|---|---|---|---|---|---|---|
| | Apple | 🙂 | 🙂 | 🙂 | 🙂 | |
| | Grapes | 🙂 | | | | |

Each 🙂 = 1 student.

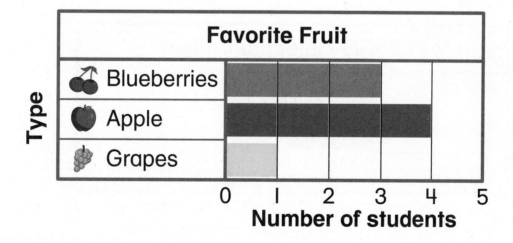

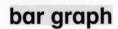

## Think and Grow

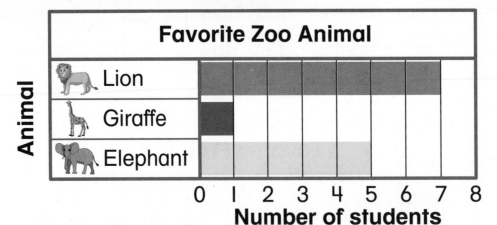

**Favorite Zoo Animal**

How many students chose elephant? __5__

Which animal is the most favorite?

## Show and Grow

1.

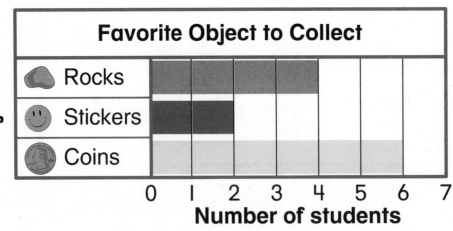

**Favorite Object to Collect**

How many students chose coins? _____

Which object is the least favorite?

## ✓ Apply and Grow: Practice

**2.**

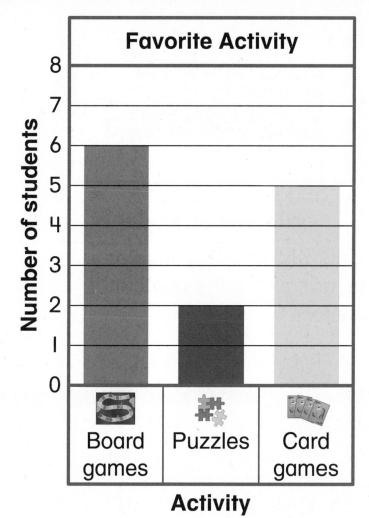

**Favorite Activity**

Number of students

Board games | Puzzles | Card games

**Activity**

How many students chose card games?

_____

How many students chose board games?

_____

Which activity is the most favorite?

---

**3.** **DIG DEEPER!** Order the activities in Exercise 2 from the most favorite to the least favorite.

_____, _____, _____

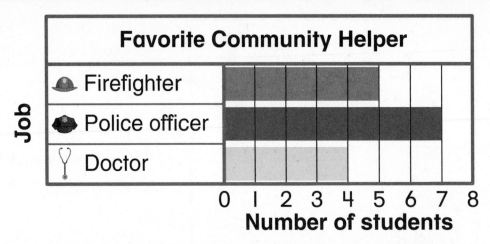

Is the number of students who chose firefighter greater than, less than, or equal to the number of students who chose doctor?

greater than     less than     equal to

## Show and Grow

4.

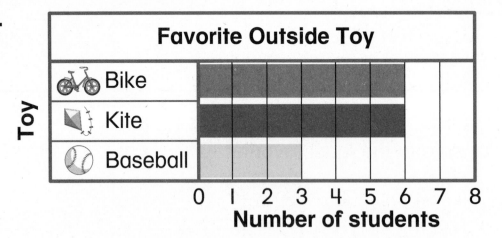

Is the number of students who chose bike greater than, less than, or equal to the number of students who chose kite?

greater than     less than     equal to

Name _____

**Learning Target:** Understand the data shown by a bar graph.

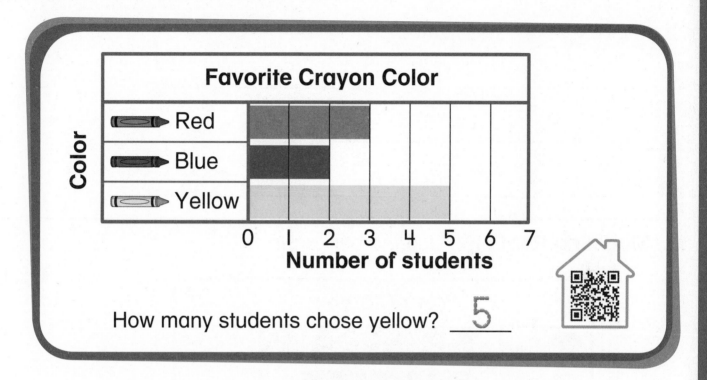

**Favorite Crayon Color**

How many students chose yellow? __5__

**I.**

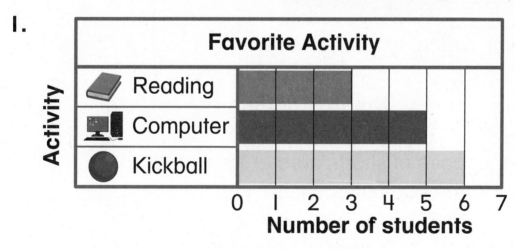

**Favorite Activity**

How many students chose reading? _____

How many students chose kickball? _____

Which activity is the least favorite?

© Big Ideas Learning, LLC

**Chapter 11** | Lesson 3

**2. Writing** How do you know which category has the most when looking at a bar graph?

_____

_____

_____

_____

**3. Modeling Real Life** Use the bar graph.

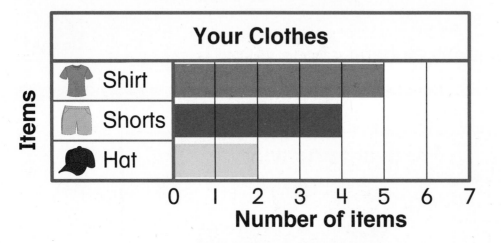

Is the number of pairs of shorts greater than, less than, or equal to the number of shirts?

greater than     less than     equal to

**Learning Target:** Make picture graphs and bar graphs.

 **Explore and Grow**

Use your color tiles to complete the tally chart and the picture graph.

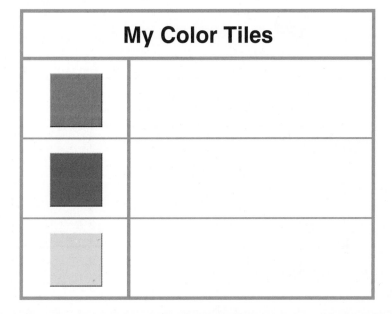

| My Color Tiles | |
|---|---|
| ■ | |
| ■ | |
| ■ | |

| Color Tiles | | | | | | | | | |
|---|---|---|---|---|---|---|---|---|---|
| ■ | | | | | | | | | |
| ■ | | | | | | | | | |
| ■ | | | | | | | | | |

Each ◯ = 1 color tile.

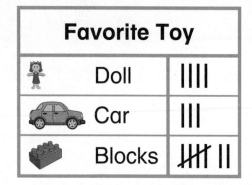

**Favorite Toy**

| | Toy | Tally |
|---|---|---|
| | Doll | IIII |
| | Car | III |
| | Blocks | IIII II |

**Favorite Toy**

| | | | | | | | | |
|---|---|---|---|---|---|---|---|---|
| Doll | ☺ | ☺ | ☺ | ☺ | | | | |
| Car | ☺ | ☺ | ☺ | | | | | |
| Blocks | ☺ | ☺ | ☺ | ☺ | ☺ | ☺ | ☺ | |

Each ☺ = I student.

# Show and Grow

**I.** Complete the bar graph.

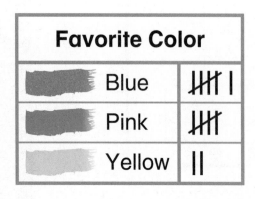

**Favorite Color**

| | Color | Tally |
|---|---|---|
| | Blue | IIII I |
| | Pink | IIII |
| | Yellow | II |

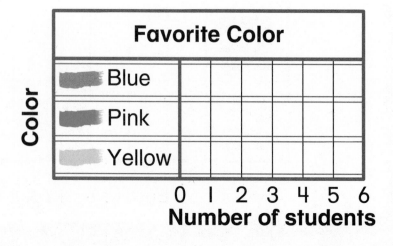

**Favorite Color**

Color

| | 0 | 1 | 2 | 3 | 4 | 5 | 6 |
|---|---|---|---|---|---|---|---|
| Blue | | | | | | | |
| Pink | | | | | | | |
| Yellow | | | | | | | |

**Number of students**

**Apply and Grow: Practice**

**2.** Complete the picture graph.

| Favorite Farm Animal | |
|---|---|
| Pig | IIII |
| Cow | HHI I |
| Horse | HHI |

| Favorite Farm Animal | | | | | | | |
|---|---|---|---|---|---|---|---|
| Pig | | | | | | | |
| Cow | | | | | | | |
| Horse | | | | | | | |

Each 🙂 = I student.

**3.** Complete the bar graph.

| Favorite Sport | |
|---|---|
| Swimming | IIII |
| Karate | II |
| Soccer | HHI |

**Favorite Sport**

| Sport | Swimming | | | | | | | |
|---|---|---|---|---|---|---|---|---|
| | Karate | | | | | | | |
| | Soccer | | | | | | | |

0 I 2 3 4 5 6 7
**Number of students**

You ask 10 students whether they are right-handed or left-handed. 2 are left-handed. The rest are right-handed. Complete the picture graph.

### How We Write

| | | | | | | | | | |
|---|---|---|---|---|---|---|---|---|---|
| 🖐 Right-handed | | | | | | | | | |
| 🖐 Left-handed | ☺ | ☺ | | | | | | | |

Each ☺ = 1 student.

## Show and Grow

**4.** You ask 11 students whether they like the swings or the slide. 5 like the swings. The rest like the slide. Complete the bar graph.

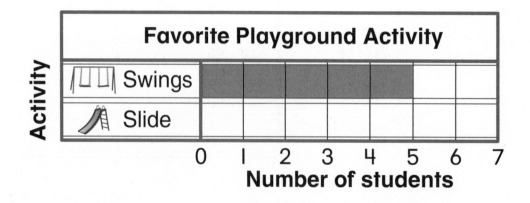

**Favorite Playground Activity**

Activity

Swings
Slide

0 1 2 3 4 5 6 7
**Number of students**

**Learning Target:** Make picture graphs and bar graphs.

| Favorite Socks | |
|---|---|
| 🧦 Black | IIII I |
| 🧦 Red | I |
| 🧦 Stripes | IIII |

| Favorite Socks | | | | | | |
|---|---|---|---|---|---|---|
| 🧦 Black | ☺ | ☺ | ☺ | ☺ | ☺ | |
| 🧦 Red | ☺ | | | | | |
| 🧦 Stripes | ☺ | ☺ | ☺ | ☺ | ☺ | |

Each ☺ = I student.

**1.** Complete the bar graph.

| Favorite Winter Activity | |
|---|---|
| 🛷 Sledding | IIII I |
| ⛸ Skating | III |
| ⛄ Snowman | IIII |

**Favorite Winter Activity**

| Activity | | | | | | | |
|---|---|---|---|---|---|---|---|
| 🛷 Sledding | | | | | | | |
| ⛸ Skating | | | | | | | |
| ⛄ Snowman | | | | | | | |

0　1　2　3　4　5　6　7
**Number of students**

**2.** Complete the picture graph.

| Balloons | |
|---|---|
| 🎈 Blue | ~~IIII~~ |
| 🎈 Red | II |

| Balloons | | | | | | |
|---|---|---|---|---|---|---|
| 🎈 Blue | | | | | | |
| 🎈 Red | | | | | | |

Each ◯ = 1 balloon.

---

**3. Modeling Real Life** You ask 8 students whether they buy or pack their lunches. 6 students buy. The rest pack. Complete the picture graph.

| Lunch Choices | | | | | | |
|---|---|---|---|---|---|---|
| 🍱 Buy | 🙂 | 🙂 | 🙂 | 🙂 | 🙂 | 🙂 |
| 💼 Pack | | | | | | |

Each 🙂 = 1 student.

~~ooooooooooooooo~~
**Review & Refresh**

Find the sum. Then change the order of the addends. Write the new equation.

**4.** $2 + 6 =$ _____

_____ + _____ = _____

**5.** _____ $= 8 + 1$

_____ $=$ _____ $+$ _____

**Learning Target:** Use data from graphs to answer questions.

## Explore and Grow

Complete the bar graph to show 19 toys in all.

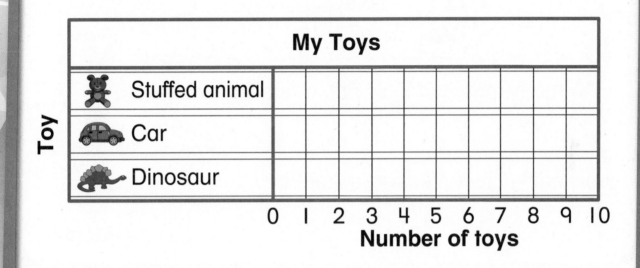

Write a question about your graph. Have your partner answer the question.

**Think and Grow**

| How You Get to School | |
|---|---|
| 🚌 Bus | ~~IIII~~ ~~IIII~~ |
| 🚶 Walk | I |
| 🚗 Car | III |

How many more students ride a bus than walk?

$\underline{10} \ominus \underline{1} = \underline{9}$     $\underline{9}$ students

How many students were asked?

$\underline{10} + \underline{1} + \underline{3} = \underline{14}$     $\underline{14}$ students

## Show and Grow

1.

| Favorite Animal That Flies | | | | | | | | |
|---|---|---|---|---|---|---|---|---|
| 🐦 Bird | 🙂 | 🙂 | 🙂 | 🙂 | 🙂 | 🙂 | | |
| 🦇 Bat | 🙂 | 🙂 | 🙂 | 🙂 | | | | |
| 🦋 Butterfly | 🙂 | 🙂 | 🙂 | 🙂 | 🙂 | 🙂 | 🙂 | |

Each 🙂 = I student.

How many more students like butterflies than birds?

_____ students

How many students were asked?     _____ students

## ✓ Apply and Grow: Practice

**2.**

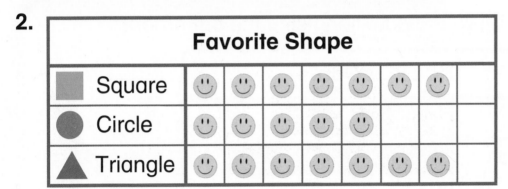

**Favorite Shape**

Each 😊 = 1 student.

How many fewer students chose circle than square?

_____ fewer students

How many students chose square or triangle?

_____ students

**3.** **DIG DEEPER!** You ask 9 students to name their favorite rainy-day activity. Complete the bar graph to show how many chose reading. Think: How do you know?

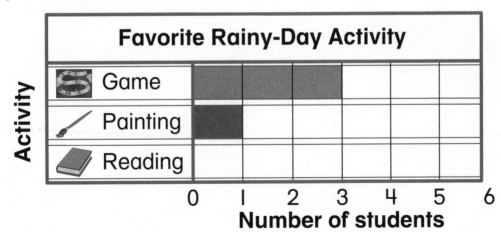

Write and answer a question using the bar graph.

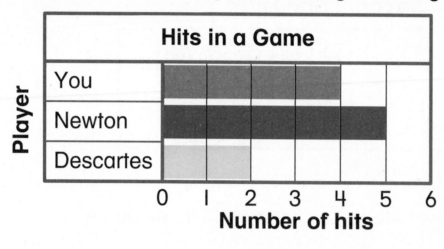

**Hits in a Game**

Player: You, Newton, Descartes

Number of hits: 0 1 2 3 4 5 6

_____

_____

_____

## Show and Grow

**4.** Write and answer a question using the tally chart.

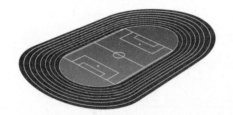

| Laps Run | |
|---|---|
| You | ‖ |
| Descartes | 卌 |
| Newton | ‖ |

_____

_____

_____

**Learning Target:** Use data from graphs to answer questions.

## My Writing Tools

| | | | | | | | |
|---|---|---|---|---|---|---|---|
| 🖍 | Marker | ○ | ○ | ○ | ○ | | |
| ✏ | Pencil | ○ | ○ | ○ | ○ | ○ | |

Each ○ = 1 writing tool.

How many writing tools do you have?

__4__ + __5__ = __9__          __9__ writing tools

**1.**

## Stuffed Animals

**Animal**

| | | | | | | | | |
|---|---|---|---|---|---|---|---|---|
| 🐻 Bear | | | | | | | | |
| 🐧 Penguin | | | | | | | | |
| 🐶 Dog | | | | | | | | |

0   1   2   3   4   5   6   7   8
**Number of stuffed animals**

How many more dogs are there than penguins?

_____ more dogs

How many bears and dogs are there in all?

_____ bears and dogs

2. **DIG DEEPER!** You ask 19 students to name their favorite fruit. Complete the tally chart to show how many chose apples. Explain how you know.

| Favorite Fruit | | |
|---|---|---|
| 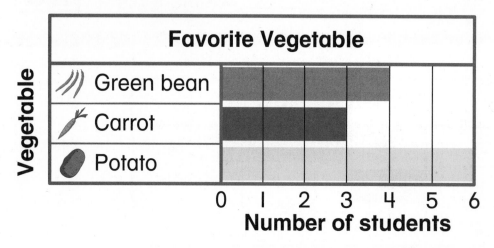 Apple | | |
| Banana | ЖЖ II | |
| Orange | II | |

_____

_____

_____

3. **Modeling Real Life** Write and answer a question using the bar graph.

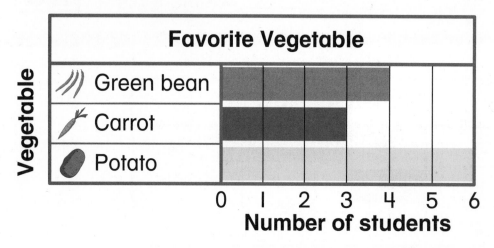

_____

_____

_____

**Review & Refresh**

4. $51 + 40 =$ _____

5. $76 + 3 =$ _____

# Performance Task

**1.** Ask your classmates about their eye colors. Use your data to complete the tally chart.

| Eye Color | |
|---|---|
| 👁 | |
| 👁 | |
| 👁 | |

**2.** Use your tally chart to complete the bar graph.

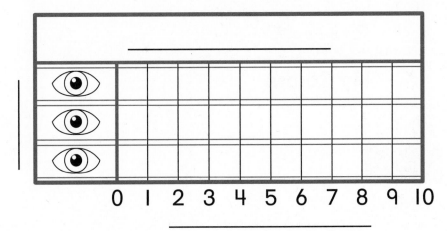

**3.** Describe two ways to tell how many students you asked.

_____

_____

**4.** Write and answer a question about your graphs.

_____

_____

# Spin and Graph

**To Play:** Spin 10 times. Complete the tally chart. Then complete the bar graph. Answer the Spin and Graph Questions about your graph.

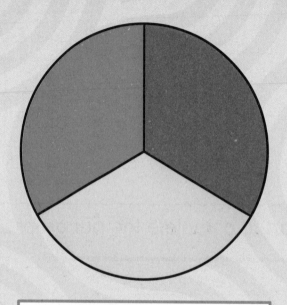

## My Colors

| | |
|---|---|
| Pink | |
| Blue | |
| Yellow | |

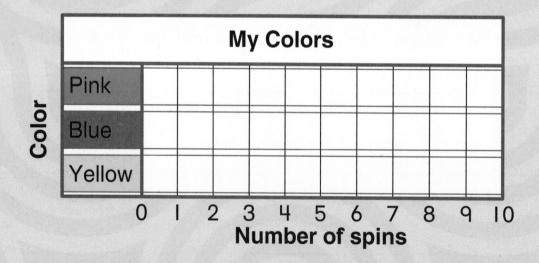

### 11.1 Sort and Organize Data

Complete the tally chart.

1.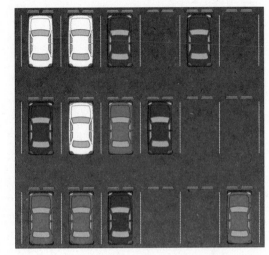

| Cars | |
|---|---|
| 🚗 Red | |
| 🚗 White | |
| 🚗 Blue | |

2.

| Pets | |
|---|---|
| 🐱 Cat | |
| 🐕 Dog | |
| 🐟 Fish | |

## 11.2  Read and Interpret Picture Graphs

**3.**

| Favorite School Subject | | | | | | | |
|---|---|---|---|---|---|---|---|
|  Art | ☺ | ☺ | ☺ | ☺ | ☺ | | |
|  Math | ☺ | ☺ | ☺ | ☺ | ☺ | ☺ | |
|  Science | ☺ | ☺ | ☺ | ☺ | | | |

Each ☺ = 1 student.

How many students chose science? _____

Which subject is the least favorite?

---

## 11.3  Read and Interpret Bar Graphs

**4.**

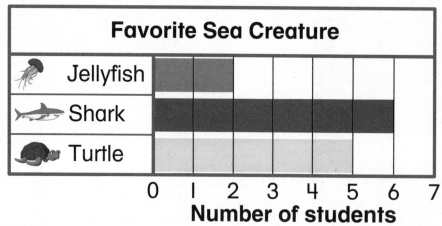

How many students chose turtle? _____

Which is the most favorite sea creature?

**5.** Complete the bar graph.

| Beads | |
|---|---|
| ● Blue | ⦀⦀ |
| ● Red | ‖ |
| ○ Yellow | ‖‖ |

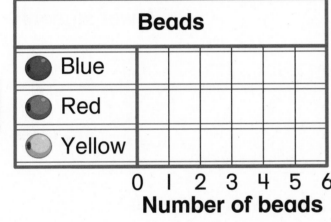

**Beads**

Color

Blue

Red

Yellow

0  1  2  3  4  5  6
**Number of beads**

**6. Modeling Real Life** You ask 13 students whether they like volleyball or basketball. 7 like volleyball. The rest like basketball. Complete the picture graph.

| Favorite Sport | | | | | | | | |
|---|---|---|---|---|---|---|---|---|
| 🏐 Volleyball | ☺ | ☺ | ☺ | ☺ | ☺ | ☺ | ☺ | |
| 🏀 Basketball | | | | | | | | |

Each ☺ = 1 student.

**7.**

| Favorite Color | |
|---|---|
| ■ Purple | 卌 \|\|\|\| |
| ■ Green | 卌 |
| ▢ Orange | \|\| |

How many fewer students chose green than purple?

_____ fewer students

How many students were asked?

_____ students

---

**8. Modeling Real Life** Write and answer a question using the bar graph.

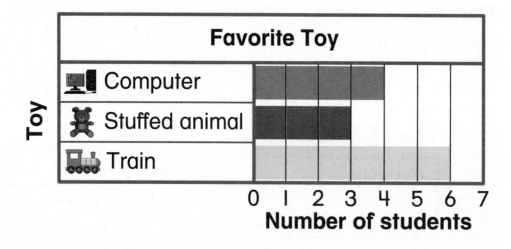

Favorite Toy

_____

_____

Name ____________________

# Cumulative Practice 1–11

**1.** Match each number on the left with a number that is 10 more.

| | |
|---|---|
| 110 | 102 |
| 92 | 22 |
| 40 | 120 |
| 12 | 50 |

**2.** Complete.

56 + 6

56 + ◯ + ◯

60 + ◯

56 + 6 = ____

**3.** Order from shortest to longest.

blue
yellow
red


________, ________, ________

**4.** Shade the circle next to the number that tells how many horns there are.

| Instruments | | |
|---|---|---|
| 🥁 | Drum | ||| |
| 📯 | Horn | 卌 卌 |
| 🔔 | Bell | 卌 | |

○ 3    ○ 10

○ 6    ○ 19

---

**5.** Shade the circle next to the sum.

$12 + 5 =$ _____

○ 15    ○ 17

○ 16    ○ 7

---

**6.** There are 85 pages in a book. You read 10 of them. How many pages are left?

○ 95    ○ 85

○ 75    ○ 80

**7.** Is each sentence true?

52 is greater than 36.          Yes          No

100 < 90                        Yes          No

75 is less than 57.             Yes          No

89 > 81                         Yes          No

---

**8.** You collect 22 cans for a food drive. Your friend collects 36. How many cans do you and your friend collect in all?

_____ cans

---

**9.** Measure.

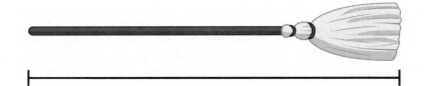

about _____ color tiles

**10.** Shade the circles next to the choices that match the model.

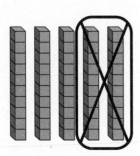

○ 50 − 30

○ 5 tens − 2 tens

○ 50 − 20

○ 3 tens − 2 tens

**11.**

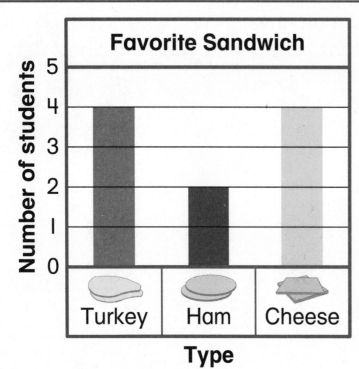

How many students chose ham? _____

Which sandwich is the least favorite?

**12.** Use each card once to write an addition equation.

_____ + _____ = _____

# 12

# Tell Time

**Chapter Learning Target:**
Understand time.

**Chapter Success Criteria:**
- I can identify numbers on a clock.
- I can explain how to tell time to the hour.
- I can compare different times on the clock.
- I can draw to show the time.

- Have you ever been on a field trip?

- Where would you like to go? How long does it take to get there?

# 12 Vocabulary

## Organize It

Use the review words to complete the graphic organizer.

## Define It

Use your vocabulary cards to identify the word.

**1.**

**2.**

**3.**

**4.**

# Chapter 12 Vocabulary Cards

analog clock

digital clock

half hour

half past

hour

hour hand

minute

minute hand

half past 3

A half hour is 30 minutes.

An hour is 60 minutes.

60 minutes is 1 hour.

# Chapter 12 Vocabulary Cards

o'clock

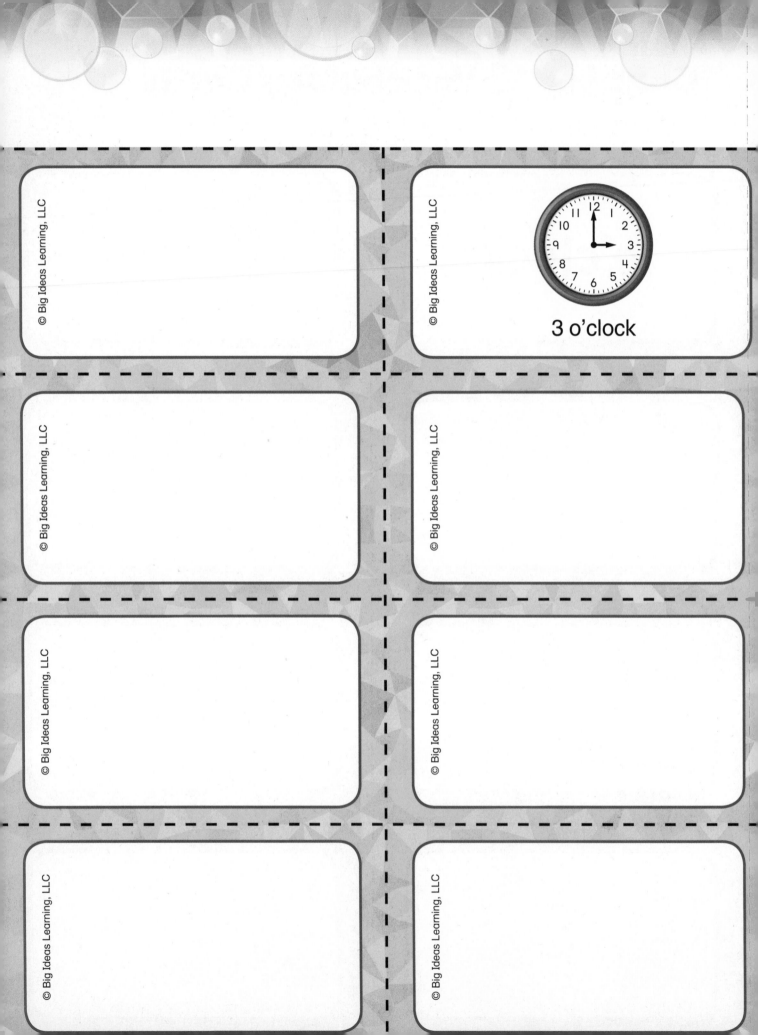

3 o'clock

**Learning Target:** Use the hour
hand to tell time to the hour.

 **Explore and Grow**

Write the missing numbers.

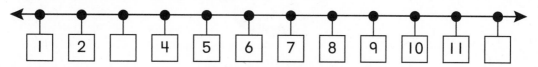

| 1 | 2 |  | 4 | 5 | 6 | 7 | 8 | 9 | 10 | 11 | |

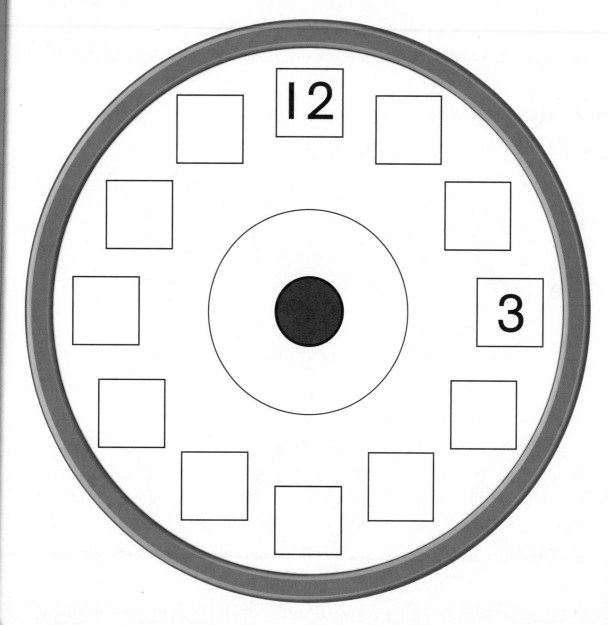

## Think and Grow

**analog clock**

An **hour** passes when the **hour hand** moves from one number to the next.

It is ___2___ **o'clock**.

## Show and Grow

Write the time shown by the hour hand.

**1.**

_____ o'clock

**2.**

_____ o'clock

**3.**

_____ o'clock

**4.**

_____ o'clock

**5.**

_____ o'clock

**6.**

_____ o'clock

## Apply and Grow: Practice

Write the time shown by the hour hand.

**7.**

_____ o'clock

**8.**

_____ o'clock

**9.**

_____ o'clock

Draw the hour hand to show the time.

**10.** 5 o'clock

**11.** 10 o'clock

**12.** 2 o'clock

**13.** **MP Precision** You wake up at 7 o'clock. Which clock shows the time you wake up?

You eat dinner I hour later than your friend. Show and write the time you eat dinner.

Friend

You

_____ o'clock

## Show and Grow

**14.** Math class starts I hour earlier than science class. Show and write the time math class starts.

Science Class

Math Class

_____ o'clock

**Learning Target:** Use the hour hand to tell time to the hour.

An hour passes when the hour hand moves from one number to the next.

_3_ o'clock.

## Write the time shown by the hour hand.

**1.**

_____ o'clock

**2.**

_____ o'clock

**3.**

_____ o'clock

## Draw the hour hand to show the time.

**4.**   4 o'clock

**5.**   12 o'clock

**6.**   8 o'clock

**7.** 🔵 **Precision** You eat a snack at 2 o'clock. Which clock shows the time you eat a snack?

---

**8.** **Modeling Real Life** Your friend gets on the bus 1 hour later than you. Show and write the time your friend gets on the bus.

You

Friend

\_\_\_\_\_ o'clock

**9.**   6 − ? = 4

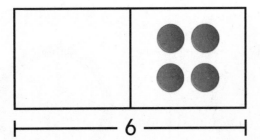

6

6 − \_\_\_\_ = 4

**10.**   8 − ? = 3

3

8

8 − \_\_\_\_ = 3

**Learning Target:** Use the hour hand to tell time to the half hour.

**Explore and Grow**

Draw the hour hand and tell the time.

The hour hand points to the 3.

It is _____ o'clock.

The hour hand points between the 3 and the 4.

It is half past _____.

The hour hand is halfway between the 1 and the 2.

So, it is **half past** _____.

A **half hour** passes when the hour hand moves halfway to the next number.

## Show and Grow

Write the time shown by the hour hand.

**1.**

half past _____

**2.**

half past _____

**3.**

half past _____

**4.**

half past _____

**5.**

half past _____

**6.**

half past _____

## ✓ Apply and Grow: Practice

Write the time shown by the hour hand.

**7.**

half past _____

**8.**

half past _____

**9.**

_____ o'clock

Draw the hour hand to show the time.

**10.** half past 6

**11.** 1 o'clock

**12.** half past 9

**13.** **DIG DEEPER!** Is it time for lunch or recess?

Lunch: half past 11
Recess: half past 12

Lunch          Recess

Soccer practice lasts a half hour. Show and circle the time practice ends.

Start               End

half past 3     5 o'clock     half past 4

## Show and Grow

**14.** A television show lasts a half hour. Show and circle the time the show ends.

Start               End

7 o'clock     half past 7     6 o'clock

A half hour passes when the hour hand moves halfway to the next number.

half past __3__

## Write the time shown by the hour hand.

**1.**

half past _____

**2.**

half past _____

**3.**

half past _____

## Draw the hour hand to show the time.

**4.** half past 9

**5.** half past 2

**6.** 10 o'clock

**7.** **DIG DEEPER!** Is it time for art class or math class?

Art class: half past 9
Math class: half past 10

Art class          Math class

---

**8.** **Modeling Real Life** Your music class lasts a half hour. Show and circle the time your music class ends.

Start                                    End

half past 12          half past 1          2 o'clock

**9.** Your friend has 9 peanuts. You have 2 fewer than your friend. How many peanuts do you have?

Friend: [                    ]

You: [                ]

_____ ◯ _____ = _____

_____ peanuts

**Learning Target:** Use the hour and minute hands to tell time to the hour and half hour.

 **Explore and Grow**

Complete the sentences.

The hour hand points to the _____.

The minute hand points to the _____.

It is _____ o'clock.

The hour hand points halfway between

the _____ and the _____.

The minute hand points to the _____.

It is half past _____.

The **minute hand** is longer than the hour hand. It shows the **minute**.

4 o'clock          half past 4

## Show and Grow

Write the time.

**1.**

_____

**2.**

_____

**3.**

_____

**4.**

_____

**5.**

_____

**6.**

_____

## ✓ Apply and Grow: Practice

Draw to show the time.

**7.** half past 5

**8.** 6 o'clock

**9.** half past 10

**10.** 3 o'clock

**11.** 11 o'clock

**12.** half past 4

---

**13.** **YOU BE THE TEACHER** Newton shows half past 6.
Is he correct? Explain.

_____

_____

_____

_____

© Big Ideas Learning, LLC

You spend an hour at the park.
Show and write the time you leave.

Arrive   Leave

_____

# Show and Grow

**14.** You spend a half hour on your homework.
Show and write the time you finish.

Start   Finish

_____

598  five hundred ninety-eight

**Learning Target:** Use the hour and minute hands to tell time to the hour and half hour.

8 o'clock          half past 8

## Write the time.

**1.**

_____

**2.**

_____

**3.**

_____

## Draw to show the time.

**4.**  5 o'clock

**5.**  half past 7

**6.**  half past 2

**7. YOU BE THE TEACHER** Descartes shows 12 o'clock.
Is he correct? Explain.

_____

_____

_____

_____

**8. Modeling Real Life** You play tag for an hour.
Show and write the time you stop playing tag.

Start                    Stop

_____

**9.** Circle the cube. Draw a rectangle around
the sphere.

**Learning Target:** Use analog and digital clocks to tell time.

 **Explore and Grow**

Show the time on the analog clock. What is the same about the clocks? What is different?

The time is _____ o'clock.

The time is half past _____.

# Think and Grow

A half hour is 30 minutes.

An hour is 60 minutes.

5:00

5:30

↑

**digital clock**

6:00

## Show and Grow

Show the time.

**1.**

**2.**

**3.**

**4.**

## ✓ Apply and Grow: Practice

Show the time.

**5.**

**6.**

Draw to show the time.

**7.**

**8.**

**DIG DEEPER!** Complete the clocks to show the same time.

**9.**

**10.**

**11. Which One Doesn't Belong?** Which time does not belong with the other three? Think: How do you know?

half past 3

© Big Ideas Learning, LLC

A play starts I hour later than a movie. Show and circle the time the play starts.

Movie

Play

half past 2          half past 4          3 o'clock          4 o'clock

## Show and Grow

12. Tumbling starts a half hour later than dance. Show and circle the time tumbling starts.

Dance

`5:00`

Tumbling

half past 5          4 o'clock          6 o'clock          half past 4

Practice **12.4**

**Learning Target:** Use analog and digital clocks to tell time.

## Show the time.

**1.**

**2.**

**3.**

## Draw to show the time.

**4.**

**5.**

**6.**

**7. Which One Doesn't Belong?** Which time does not belong with the other three? Think: How do you know?

   half past 6

**8. Modeling Real Life** Bowling starts 1 hour later than ice skating. Show and circle the time bowling starts.

Ice Skating                    Bowling

half past 5        5 o'clock        half past 4        3 o'clock

**Review & Refresh**

**9.** Circle the cone. Draw a rectangle around the cylinder.

**1.** Your class is on a field trip to a nature center. Complete the schedule.

**a.** The Pond Study starts at the time shown.

**b.** The Wildlife Walk starts at half past 9.

**c.** The Scavenger Hunt starts 1 hour after the Wildlife Walk starts.

**d.** Recess starts a half hour after lunch.

**e.** You leave 1 hour before 3:00.

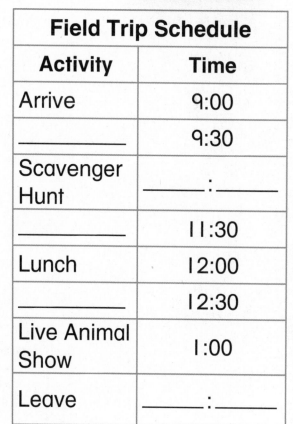

| Field Trip Schedule | |
|---|---|
| **Activity** | **Time** |
| Arrive | 9:00 |
| _____ | 9:30 |
| Scavenger Hunt | ____ : ____ |
| _____ | 11:30 |
| Lunch | 12:00 |
| _____ | 12:30 |
| Live Animal Show | 1:00 |
| Leave | ____ : ____ |

**2.** Lunch lasts a half hour. Write the time that lunch ends.

**3.** Draw the time the Live Animal Show starts.

# Time Flip and Find

**To Play:** Place the Time Flip and Find Cards facedown in the boxes. Take turns flipping 2 cards. If your cards show the same time, keep the cards. If your cards show different times, flip the cards back over. Play until all matches are made.

# Chapter Practice 12

## 12.1 Tell Time to the Hour

Write the time shown by the hour hand.

**1.**

_____ o'clock

**2.**

_____ o'clock

**3.**

_____ o'clock

## 12.2 Tell Time to the Half Hour

Draw the hour hand to show the time.

**4.** half past 9

**5.** 2 o'clock

**6.** half past 5

**7.** **MP** **Precision** Is it time to brush your teeth or go to bed?

Brush teeth: half past 7
Go to bed: half past 8

Brush teeth

Go to bed

## 12.3 Tell Time to the Hour and Half Hour

Write the time.

**8.**

_____

**9.**

_____

**10.**

_____

**11. Modeling Real Life** You read for a half hour.
Show and write the time you stop reading.

Start

Stop

_____

## 12.4 Tell Time Using Analog and Digital Clocks

Complete the clocks to show the same time.

**12.**

**13.**

**14.**

# 13

# Two- and Three- Dimensional Shapes

- Have you ever built a sandcastle?
- What shapes do you see?

**Chapter Learning Target:**
Understand two- and three-dimensional shapes.

**Chapter Success Criteria:**
- I can identify shapes.
- I can describe two- and three-dimensional shapes.
- I can compare shapes.
- I can create shapes.

# 13 Vocabulary

**Review Words**
hexagon
square

## Organize It

Use the review words to complete the graphic organizer.

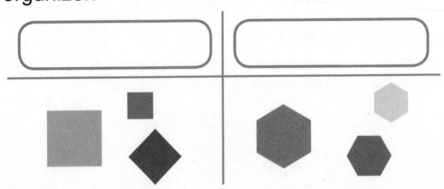

## Define It

Use your vocabulary cards to identify the words. Find each word in the word search.

1.

2.

3.

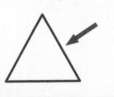

```
T  F  S  P  E  Z  U  I  D
Y  H  I  P  D  I  R  E  L
V  O  D  U  Z  S  V  P  D
E  M  E  H  O  L  B  A  S
R  R  I  L  M  C  K  U  T
T  U  K  S  F  T  O  T  K
E  S  U  L  Z  F  A  C  B
X  I  S  F  N  C  E  R  U
D  M  E  D  G  E  T  S  N
```

# Chapter 13 Vocabulary Cards

curved surface

edge

flat surface

rectangular prism

rhombus

side

three-dimensional shape

trapezoid

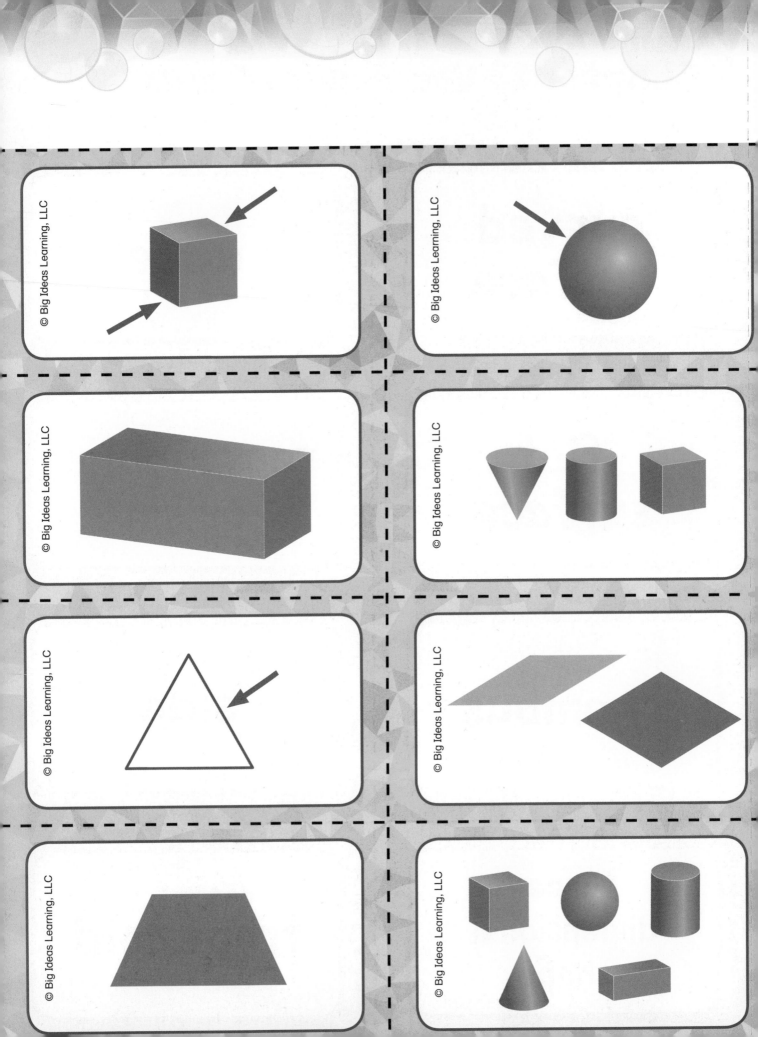

two-dimensional
shape

vertex

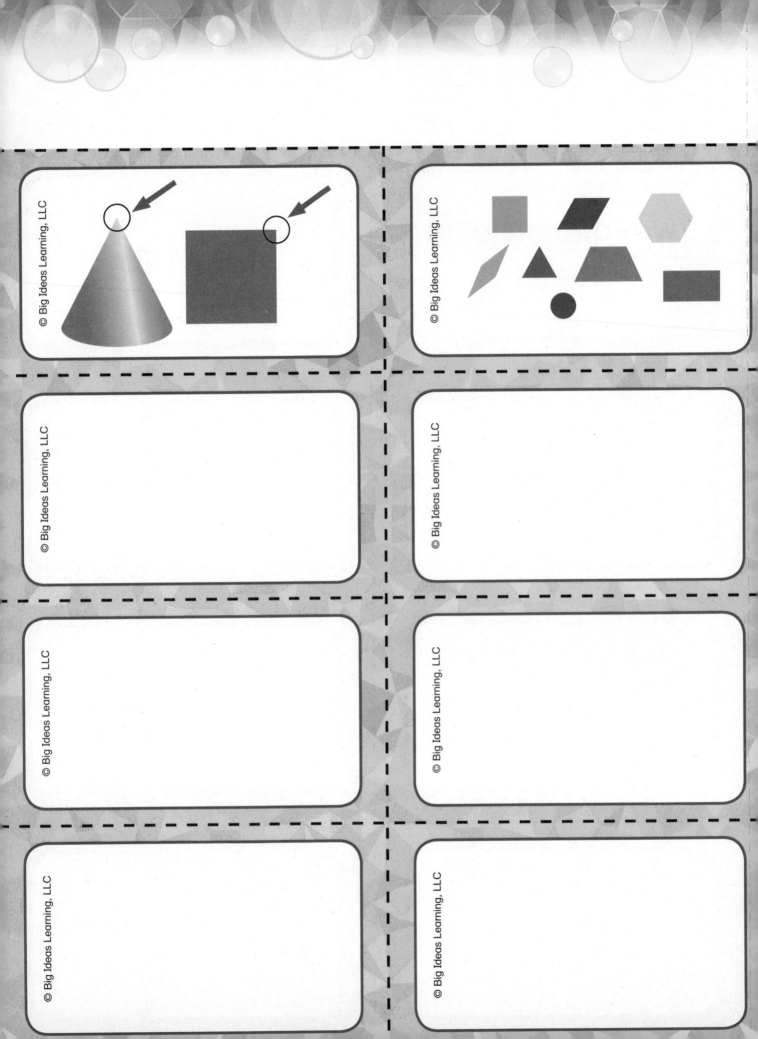

**Learning Target:** Sort two-dimensional shapes.

 **Explore and Grow**

Sort the Shape Sort Cards. Explain how you sorted.

You can sort **two-dimensional shapes** in many ways.

| **Closed or Open** | **Number of Sides** | **Number of Vertices** |
|---|---|---|
| Closed  |  sides |  vertices |
| Open 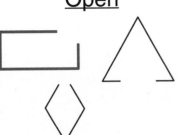 | side  | vertex 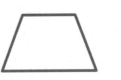 |

## Show and Grow

1. Circle the closed shapes with 4 vertices.

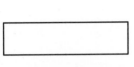 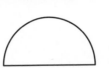

2. Circle the closed shapes with no straight sides.

## Apply and Grow: Practice

**3.** Circle the closed shapes with only 3 vertices.

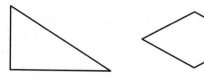
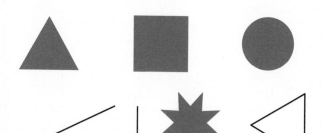

**4.** Circle the closed shapes with only L-shaped vertices.

**5.** Circle the shapes with more than 4 straight sides.

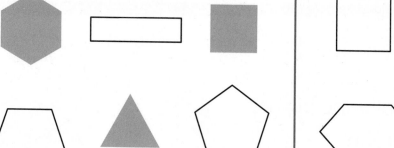

**6.** Circle the shapes with 6 straight sides.

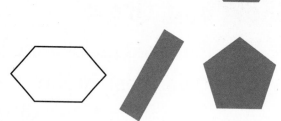

**7.** **DIG DEEPER!** Draw 2 different two-dimensional shapes that have only 4 straight sides.

Use the clues to color the picture.

Only 3 straight sides: **blue**          Only 4 straight sides: **green**

No straight sides: **yellow**          More than 4 vertices: **red**

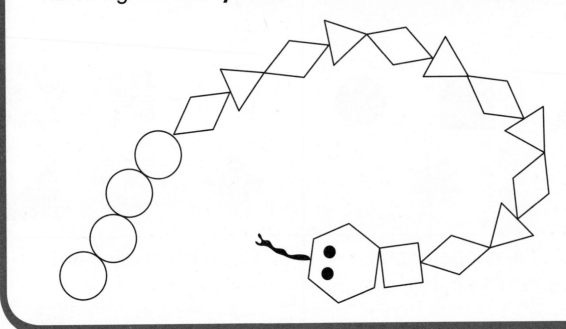

## Show and Grow

**8.** Use the clues to color the picture.

Only 3 vertices: **green**

All L-shaped vertices: **orange**

Only 4 straight sides and
     no L-shaped vertices: **blue**

6 straight sides: **yellow**

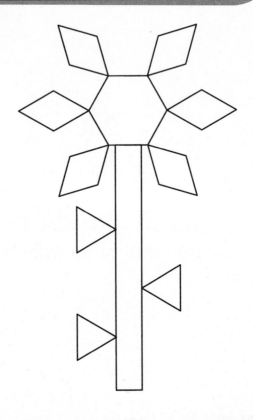

**Learning Target:** Sort two-dimensional shapes.

You can sort two-dimensional shapes in many ways.

| **Closed or Open** | **Number of Sides** | **Number of Vertices** |
|---|---|---|

Closed          Open

<u>4</u> sides

<u>3</u> vertices

**1.** Circle the closed shapes with no straight sides.

**2.** Circle the closed shapes with 4 sides of the same length.

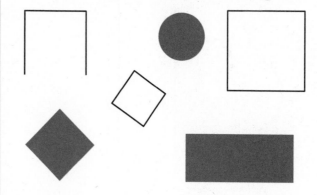

**3.** Circle the shapes with no vertices.

**4.** Circle the shapes with more than 4 vertices.

**5.** **DIG DEEPER!** Draw 2 different two-dimensional shapes with 2 long straight sides and 2 short straight sides.

---

**6. Modeling Real Life** Use the clues to color the picture.

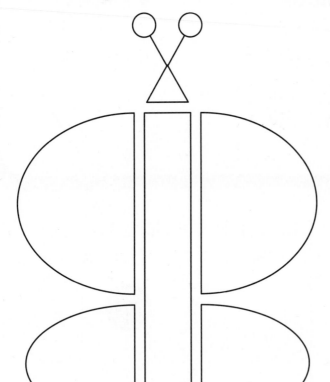

Only 3 vertices: **yellow**

Only 4 sides: **black**

Only 1 straight side: **orange**

No straight sides: **blue**

**Review & Refresh**

**7.** Circle the longer object.

**Learning Target:** Describe
two-dimensional shapes.

 **Explore and Grow**

Which shape has three sides?

Which shapes have 4 sides and 4 L-shaped vertices?

Which shapes have 4 sides and no L-shaped vertices?

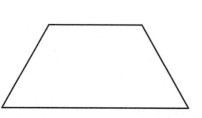 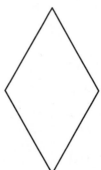 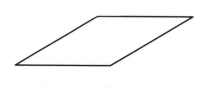

Use your materials to build each shape you circled.

triangle — _3_ straight sides — _3_ vertices

rectangle — _4_ straight sides — _4_ vertices

square — _4_ straight sides — _4_ vertices

hexagon — _6_ straight sides — _6_ vertices

**trapezoid** — _4_ straight sides — _4_ vertices

**rhombus** — _4_ straight sides — _4_ vertices

# Show and Grow

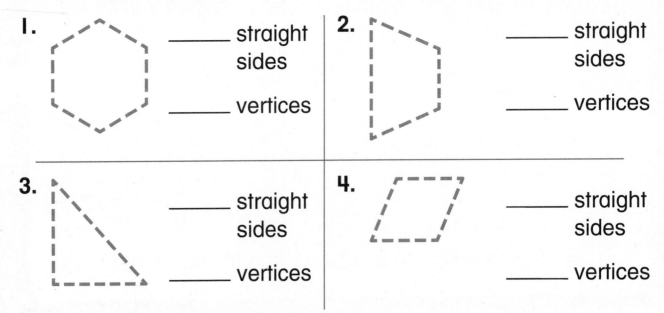

1. _____ straight sides   _____ vertices

2. _____ straight sides   _____ vertices

3. _____ straight sides   _____ vertices

4. _____ straight sides   _____ vertices

Name _____

**5.**  _____ straight sides

_____ vertices

**6.**  _____ straight sides

_____ vertices

**7.** _____ straight sides

_____ vertices

**8.**  _____ straight sides

_____ vertices

Circle the attributes of the shape.

**9.**     **Triangle**

0 straight sides

3 straight sides

3 vertices

open

**10.**     **Square**

6 straight sides of the same length

4 straight sides of the same length

4 vertices

closed

**11.** **MP Precision** Match each shape with an attribute that describes it.

| Circle | Rectangle | Hexagon |

| 6 straight sides | 0 vertices | only 4 vertices |

A board game has 4 sides and 4 L-shaped vertices. Name and draw two shapes for the board game.

Circle:   Square      Hexagon      Trapezoid      Rectangle

Draw shapes:

## Show and Grow

12. A board game has 4 sides and no L-shaped vertices. Name and draw two shapes for the board game.

Circle:   Triangle      Trapezoid      Rhombus      Square

Draw shapes:

__4__ straight sides

__4__ vertices

__3__ straight sides

__3__ vertices

**1.** _____ straight sides

_____ vertices

**2.** _____ straight sides

_____ vertices

**3.**  _____ straight sides

_____ vertices

**4.** _____ straight sides

_____ vertices

Circle the attributes of the shape.

**5.**          **Trapezoid**

4 straight sides

6 straight sides

5 vertices

closed

**6.**          **Rectangle**

4 straight sides

0 vertices

4 vertices

open

**7.** 🔵 **Precision** Match each shape with an attribute that describes it.

| Triangle | Trapezoid | Circle |

| only 3 straight sides | 0 straight sides | 4 vertices |

---

**8. Modeling Real Life** A photograph has 4 straight sides of the same length and 4 vertices. Draw and name two possible shapes for the photograph.

_____     _____

**Review & Refresh**

**9.** 🔵 **Reasoning** Which sentences are correct?

| Animals at a Petting Zoo | |
|---|---|
| 🦌 Deer | 卌 ll |
| 🐎 Pony | llll l |
| 🐐 Goat | 卌 lll |

There are 5 ponies.

There are 7 deer.

There are more goats than ponies.

The numbers of deer and goats are the same.

Name _____

**Learning Target:** Join two-dimensional shapes to make another shape.

**Explore and Grow**

Use 2 triangles to make a new two-dimensional shape. Draw your shape.

Use 3 triangles to make a new two-dimensional shape. Draw your shape.

**Think and Grow**

Use smaller shapes to make a new, larger shape.

How many  make a  ?

 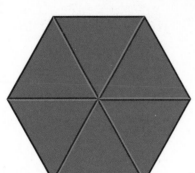

_6_  make a  .

## Show and Grow

**1.** How many  make a  ?

_____  make a  .

**2.** How many  make a  ?

_____  make a  .

**3.** How many  make a  ?

_____  make a  .

**4.** How many  make a  ?

_____  make a  .

# Apply and Grow: Practice

**5.** How many 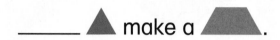 make a ◢◣ ?

_____ ▲ make a ◢◣ .

**6.** How many ◼ make a  ?

_____ ◼ make a ▬ .

**7.** Draw the shape you can use 2 times to make a  .

**8.** Draw the shape you can use 3 times to make a ⬡ .

**9.** (MP) **Choose Tools** Which shape can you use 2 times to make a ▱ ?

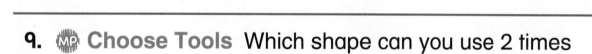

**10.** **DIG DEEPER!** Draw to show 2 different ways you can use pattern blocks to make the shape.

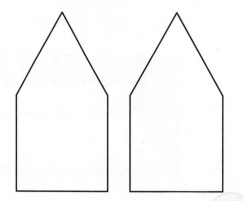

# Think and Grow: Modeling Real Life

Use the number of pattern blocks to fill the shape on the sign. How many of each block do you use? Draw to show your work.

3 blocks:

4 blocks:

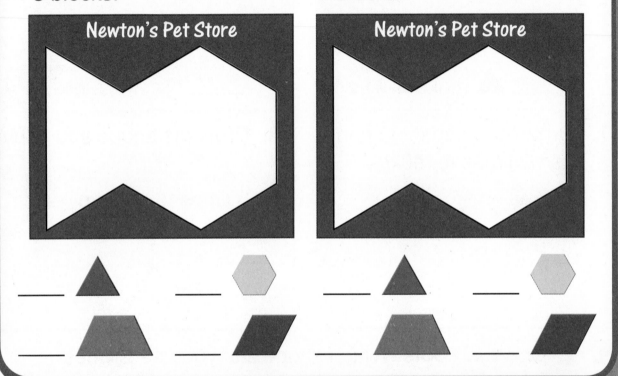

## Show and Grow

11. Use 3 pattern blocks to fill the shape on the sign. How many of each block do you use? Draw to show your work.

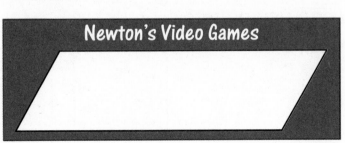

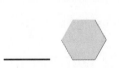

**Learning Target:** Join two-dimensional shapes to make another shape.

How many 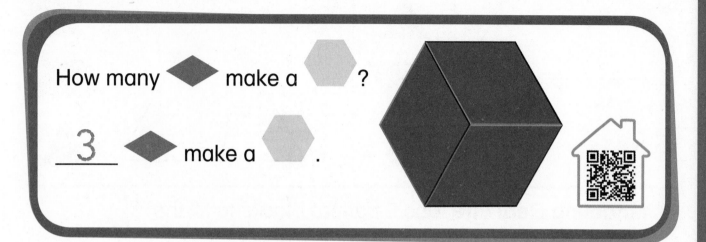 make a ?

___3___ make a .

1. How many ▲ make a ?

_____ ▲ make a  .

2. How many ╱ make a ⊲ ?

_____ ╱ make a ⊲ .

3. How many ▲ make a ?

_____ ▲ make a .

4. How many ◗ make a ◡ ?

_____ ◗ make a ◡ .

**MP** **Choose Tools** Which 2 pattern blocks can you use to make the shape?

5.

6.

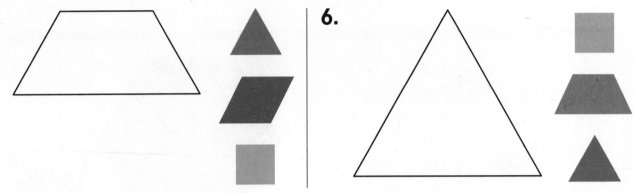

7. **Modeling Real Life** Use 5 pattern blocks to fill the shape on the sign. How many of each block do you use? Draw to show your work.

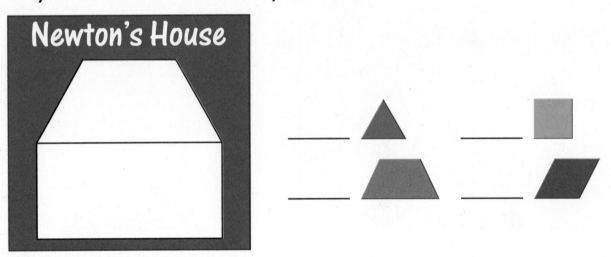

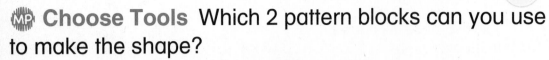

Newton's House

Review & Refresh

Write the time.

8.

9.

_____ : _____          _____ : _____

**Learning Target:** Join two-dimensional shapes to make a new shape. Use the new shape to make a larger shape.

**Explore and Grow**

Use two or more shapes to make the center of the flower. Use more shapes to fill in the rest of the flower.

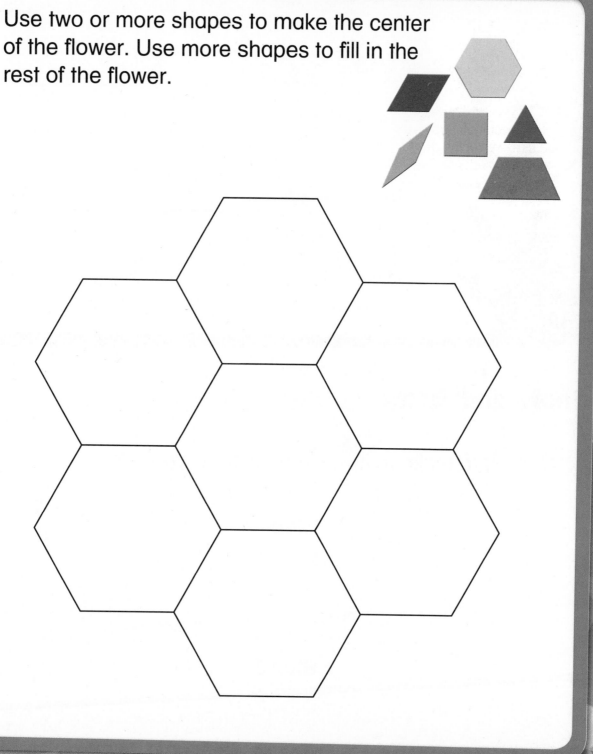

## Think and Grow

Use ◢ to make a ▪.

**Step 1** →

Make a rectangle first. Then use two rectangles to make a square.

**Step 2** →

## Show and Grow

1. Use  to make a ●. Draw to show your work.

**Step 1** →

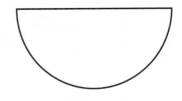

**Step 2** →

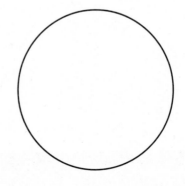

## ✓ Apply and Grow: Practice

**2.** Use 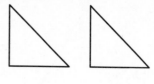 to make a ▭. Draw to show your work.

 Step 1

Step 2

**3.** Use △ and  to make a 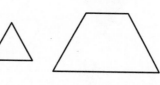. Draw to show your work.

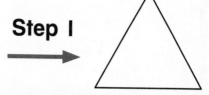 Step 1

Step 2

**4.** Draw the shape you can use 3 times to make a .

**5.** Draw the shape you can use 4 times to make a △.

**6.** **DIG DEEPER!** Draw to show two different ways you can join the shapes on the left to make the larger shape.

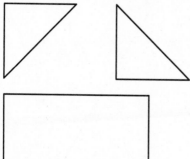

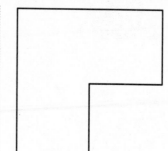

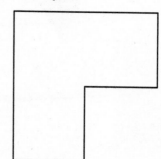

## Think and Grow: Modeling Real Life

Use pattern blocks to complete the puzzle. How many of each block do you use? Draw to show your work.

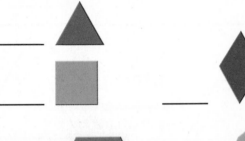

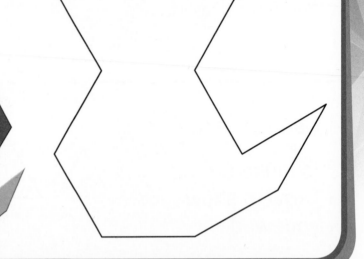

## Show and Grow

**7.** Use pattern blocks to complete the puzzle. How many of each block do you use? Draw to show your work.

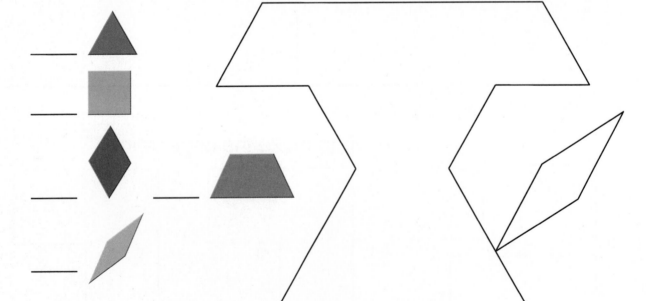

**Learning Target:** Join two-dimensional shapes to make a new shape. Use the new shape to make a larger shape.

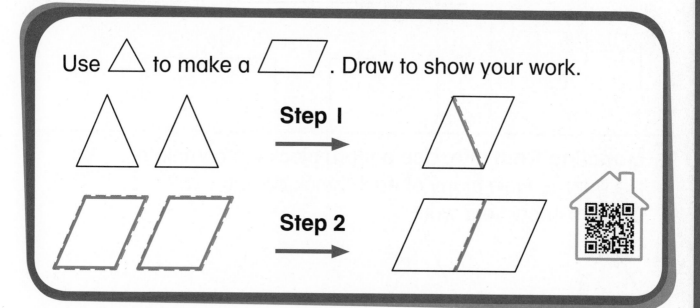

Use △ to make a ▱. Draw to show your work.

**Step 1** →

**Step 2** →

1. Use ⬜ to make a larger ⬜. Draw to show your work.

**Step 1** →

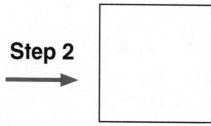

**Step 2** →

2. Use ◺ to make a ◇. Draw to show your work.

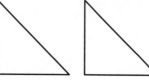

**Step 1** →

**Step 2** →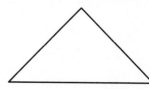

**3.** DIG DEEPER! Draw to show two ways you can combine the 3 shapes on the left to make the larger shape.

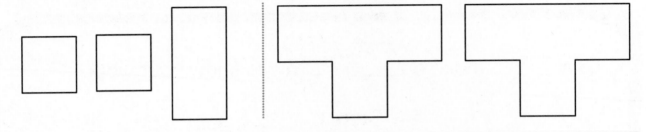

**4. Modeling Real Life** Use pattern blocks to complete the puzzle. How many of each block do you use? Draw to show your work.

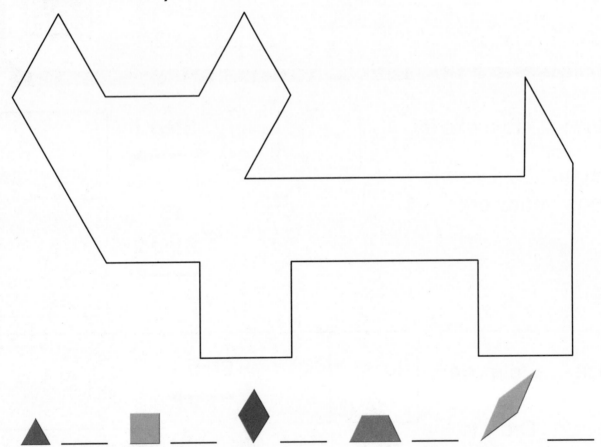

**Review & Refresh**

**5.** _____ is greater than

17                    19.

_____ is less than

**6.** _____ is greater than

12                    11.

_____ is less than

**Learning Target:** Take apart
two-dimensional shapes.

## Explore and Grow

Draw lines to take apart each figure.

Show two rectangles.

Show four squares.

Show 2 triangles
and 1 rectangle.

Show 2 triangles
and 2 squares.

Here are two more ways.

Draw one line to show 2 rectangles.

## Show and Grow

Draw one line to show the parts.

**1.** 2 triangles

**2.** 2 triangles

**3.** 2 trapezoids

**4.** 1 triangle and 1 trapezoid

## ✓ Apply and Grow: Practice

Draw one line to show the parts.

**5.** 2 triangles

**6.** 2 squares

Draw two lines to show the parts.

**7.** 2 triangles and 1 trapezoid

**8.** 2 triangles and 1 rectangle

**9.** **MP** **Reasoning** Show how to use the shapes to make the hexagon.

1

3 △

- - - - - - - - - - - - - - - - - - - - - - - -

2 ▱

2 △

**10.** **MP** **Reasoning** Show how to use the shapes to make a circle. How many of each shape do you use?

 ____    ____

How many squares can you find on the Four Square court?

_____ squares

## Show and Grow

11. How many squares can you find on the magic square?

| 2 | 7 | 6 |
|---|---|---|
| 9 | 5 | 1 |
| 4 | 3 | 8 |

_____ squares

Name _____

**Learning Target:** Take apart two-dimensional shapes.

Draw one line to show 2 triangles.

Here is another way.

Draw one line to show the parts.

**1.** 2 trapezoids

**2.** I rectangle and I square

Draw two lines to show the parts.

**3.** 3 triangles

**4.** I rectangle and 2 triangles

**5.** 🔵 **Reasoning** Show how to use the shapes to make the .

| | | |
|---|---|---|
| 1 | ▱ | |
| 2 | △ | |

| | |
|---|---|
| 1 | ⬡ |
| 1 | △ |

**6.** 🔵 **Reasoning** Show how to use the shapes to make the hexagon. How many of each shape do you use?

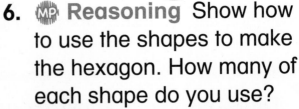

▱ _____          △ _____

**7. Modeling Real Life** How many triangles are in Descartes's design?

Geoboard!

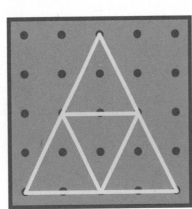

_____ triangles

**Review & Refresh**

**8.** Circle the three-dimensional shapes. Draw rectangles around the two-dimensional shapes.

**Learning Target:** Sort
three-dimensional shapes.

 **Explore and Grow**

Sort the Three-Dimensional Shape Cards. Explain
how you sorted.

© Big Ideas Learning, LLC

## Think and Grow

You can sort **three-dimensional shapes** in many ways.

**Only Flat Surfaces**

flat surface

**Only a Curved Surface**

curved surface

## Show and Grow

1. Circle the shapes with flat surfaces that are circles.

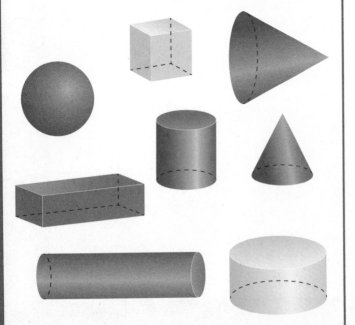

2. Circle the shapes with both flat and curved surfaces.

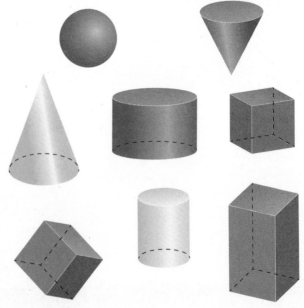

## ✓ Apply and Grow: Practice

**3.** Circle the shapes with 1 or more flat surfaces.

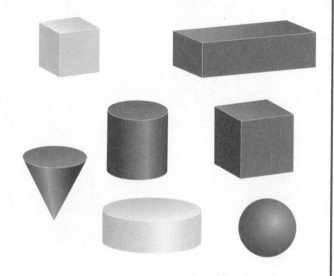

**4.** Circle the shapes with a curved surface.

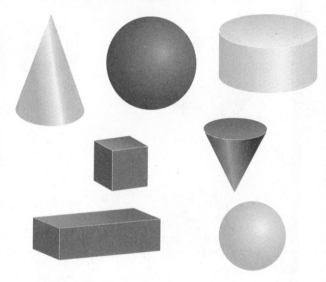

**5.** Circle the shapes with only 2 flat surfaces.

**6.** 🔘 **Structure** Match each shape to its group.

| only flat surfaces | both flat and curved surfaces | only a curved surface |

**Think and Grow: Modeling Real Life**

You need to find an object that has no flat surfaces for a scavenger hunt. Circle the objects you can use.

## Show and Grow

**7.** You need to find an object that has only two flat surfaces for a scavenger hunt. Circle the objects you can use.

**Learning Target:** Sort three-dimensional shapes.

You can sort three-dimensional shapes in many ways.

| **Flat Surfaces that are Rectangles** | **Flat Surfaces that are Circles** |
|---|---|
| 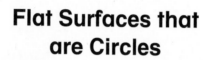 |   |

**1.** Circle the shapes with no flat surface.

**2.** Circle the shapes with flat surfaces that are rectangles.

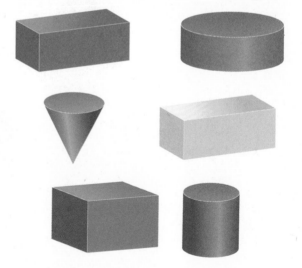

**3.** Circle the shapes with more than 2 flat surfaces.

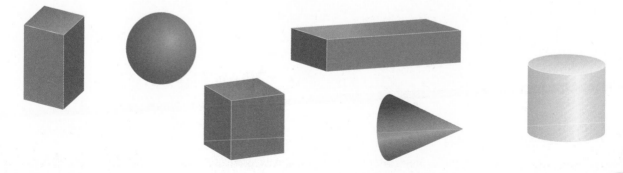

**4.**  **Structure** Match each shape to its group.

| only 1 flat surface | no flat surfaces | more than 1 flat surface |
|:---:|:---:|:---:|

**5. Modeling Real Life** You need to find an object that has both flat and curved surfaces for a scavenger hunt. Circle the objects you can use.

**Review & Refresh**

**6.** 30 + 30 = _____

**7.** 60 + 20 = _____

**8.** 50 + 10 = _____

**9.** 30 + 40 = _____

**Explore and Grow**

Use your materials to build one of the three-dimensional shapes shown. Circle the shape you make. How many flat surfaces does your shape have? How many vertices does your shape have?

_____ flat surfaces

_____ vertices

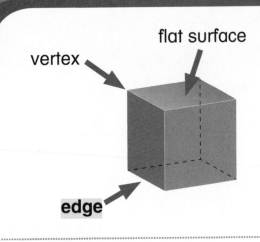

vertex

flat surface

**edge**

cube

__6__ flat surfaces

__8__ vertices

__12__ edges

**rectangular prism**

__6__ flat surfaces

__8__ vertices

__12__ edges

cylinder

__2__ flat surfaces

__0__ vertices

__0__ edges

cone

__1__ flat surface

__1__ vertices

__0__ edges

sphere

__0__ flat surfaces

__0__ vertices

__0__ edges

## Show and Grow

1.

____ flat surfaces   ____ vertices

____ edges

Name _____

**2.**  _____ flat surfaces

_____ vertices

_____ edges

**3.**  _____ flat surfaces

_____ vertices

_____ edges

Circle the attributes of the shape.

**4.** **Cone**

1 flat surface

0 vertices

slides

two-dimensional

**5.** **Cube**

6 flat surfaces

12 vertices

12 edges

rolls

**6.** I am a three-dimensional shape that has no flat surfaces, no vertices, and no edges. What am I?

_____

**7.** I am a three-dimensional shape that has 1 flat surface, 1 vertex, and no edges. What am I?

_____

**8.** **DIG DEEPER!** Newton buys an item that has 2 more flat surfaces than edges. Which item does he buy?

# Think and Grow: Modeling Real Life

Circle the object below the table that has 0 flat surfaces. Draw a line through the object above the basketball that has 12 edges.

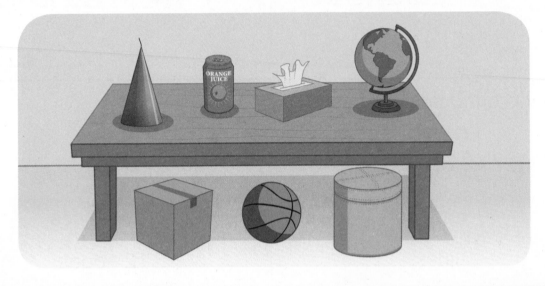

## Show and Grow

9. Circle the object in front of the campers that has more than 2 flat surfaces. Draw a line through the object behind the logs that has 1 vertex and 1 flat surface.

**Learning Target:** Describe three-dimensional shapes.

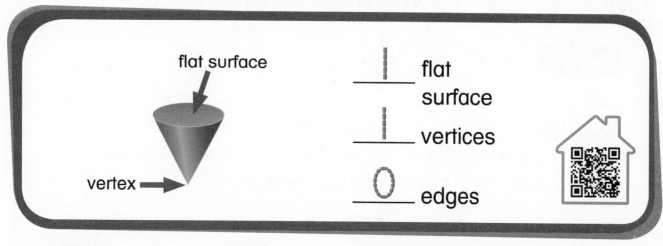

flat surface

vertex ➡

_____ | flat surface

_____ | vertices

_____ 0 edges

**1.**  _____ flat surfaces

_____ vertices

_____ edges

**2.** _____ flat surfaces

_____ vertices

_____ edges

**3.** Circle the shape that has the same number of vertices as edges.

**4.** Circle the shape that has the same number of faces as vertices.

Circle the attributes of the shape.

**5.** **Cylinder**

2 flat surfaces

3 flat surfaces

2 vertices

stacks

**6.** **Rectangular Prism**

8 flat surfaces

12 edges

slides

three-dimensional

**7.** **DIG DEEPER!** Descartes buys an item that has 2 fewer flat surfaces than vertices. Which item does he buy?

**8.** **Modeling Real Life** Circle the object next to the hat that has 6 square flat surfaces. Draw a line through the object in front of the hat that has 0 edges and 1 vertex.

**9.** $20 + 18 = $ _____

**10.** $40 + 25 = $ _____

**11.** $36 + 60 = $ _____

**12.** $9 + 90 = $ _____

**13.** $18 + 70 = $ _____

**14.** $27 + 50 = $ _____

## Explore and Grow

Which three-dimensional shapes can you make using cubes? Build one of the shapes.

## Think and Grow

Use the rectangular prisms to make a new shape.

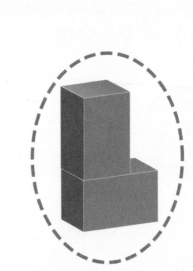

## Show and Grow

Circle the new shape that you can make.

**1.**

**2.**

**Apply and Grow: Practice**

Circle the new shape that you can make.

**3.**

  |

**4.**

  |

**5.**

  |

**6.** **DIG DEEPER!** How many cubes do you need in all to make the next shape?

     ?

_____ cubes

You build a wall. It is 5 cubes long and 2 cubes tall. Your friend builds a wall. It is 4 cubes long and 2 cubes tall. How many more cubes do you use than your friend?

Draw pictures: <u>You</u>          <u>Friend</u>

Equation:

_____ more cubes

## Show and Grow

7. You build a wall. It is 3 cubes long and 3 cubes tall. Your friend builds a wall. It is 5 cubes long and 3 cubes tall. How many more cubes does your friend use than you?

Draw pictures: <u>You</u>          <u>Friend</u>

Equation:

_____ more cubes

**Practice** **13.8**

Circle the new shape that you can make.

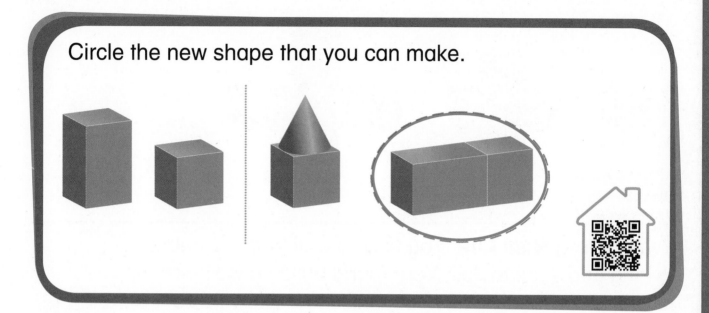

Circle the new shape that you can make.

**1.**

**2.**

**3.** **DIG DEEPER!** How many cubes do you need in all to make the next shape?

? 

_____ cubes

**4.** **Modeling Real Life** You build a wall that is 2 cubes long and 4 cubes tall. Your friend builds a wall that is 4 cubes long and 3 cubes tall. How many more cubes does your friend use than you?

_____ more cubes

**Review & Refresh**

**5.** Order from shortest to longest.

green

yellow

black

_____, _____, _____

**Learning Target:** Take apart three-dimensional shapes.

 **Explore and Grow**

Circle the three-dimensional shapes used to build the castle.

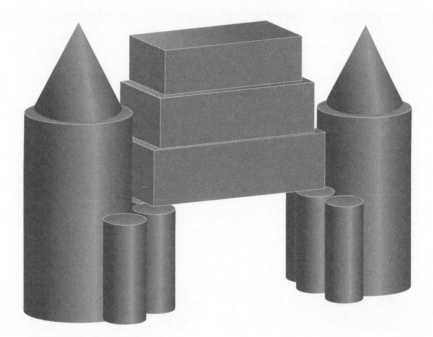

# Think and Grow

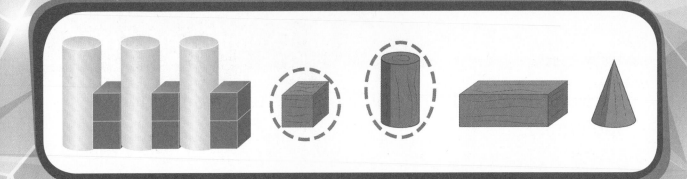

## Show and Grow

Circle the shapes that make up the structure.

**1.**

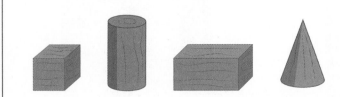

**2.**

**3.**

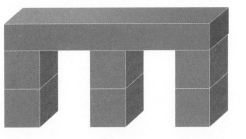

**4.**

## ✓ Apply and Grow: Practice

Circle the shapes that make up the structure.

**5.**

**6.**

**7.**

**8.**

**9.** 🔵 **Reasoning** Which two structures are the same?

How many of each shape make up the gate?

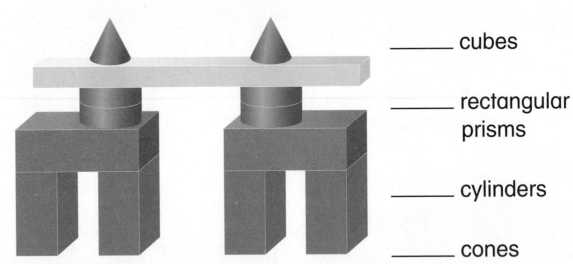

_____ cubes

_____ rectangular prisms

_____ cylinders

_____ cones

## Show and Grow

**10.** How many of each shape make up the bridge?

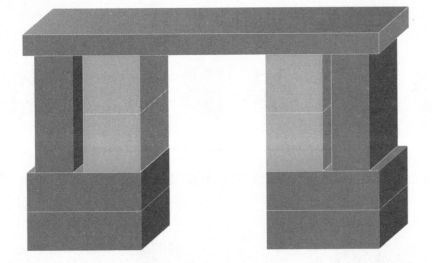

_____ cubes

_____ rectangular prisms

_____ cylinders

_____ cones

**Learning Target:** Take apart three-dimensional shapes.

Circle the shapes that make up the structure.

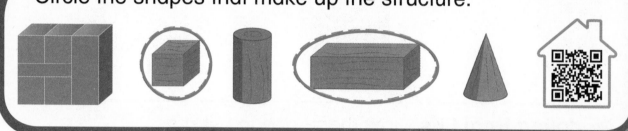

Circle the shapes that make up the structure.

**1.**

**2.**

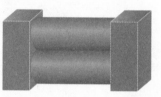

**3.**

**4.**

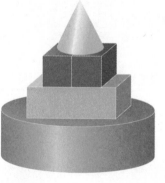

**5.**  **Reasoning** Which two structures are the same?

---

**6. Modeling Real Life** How many of each shape make up the castle?

_____ cubes

_____ rectangular
        prisms

_____ cylinders

_____ cones

**Review & Refresh**

**7.** $12 + 7 =$ _____

**8.** $42 + 14 =$ _____

**9.** $25 + 32 =$ _____

**10.** $68 + 11 =$ _____

1. Use the clues to finish the two-dimensional sand castle drawing.

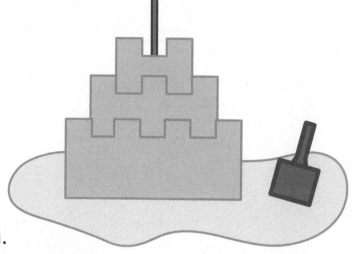

- The flag on the castle is a closed shape with only 3 straight sides.

- The handle of the shovel is a closed shape with L-shaped vertices and 4 sides of the same length.

- The window on the castle is a closed shape with only 6 straight sides.

- The door on the castle is a closed shape with 4 sides that you can use 2 times to make a square.

---

2. You are building a sand castle using these three-dimensional shapes.

- 4 shapes that have square flat surfaces

- 5 shapes that have 2 flat surfaces and no vertices

- 3 shapes that have the same number of flat surfaces as vertices

a. Which shape is missing from the sand castle?

b. Color a flat surface to show where you would stack the missing shape to complete the sand castle.

# Shape Roll and Build

**To Play:** Roll a die to choose a pattern block. Cover a shape in the picture. Keep rolling until all shapes have been covered.

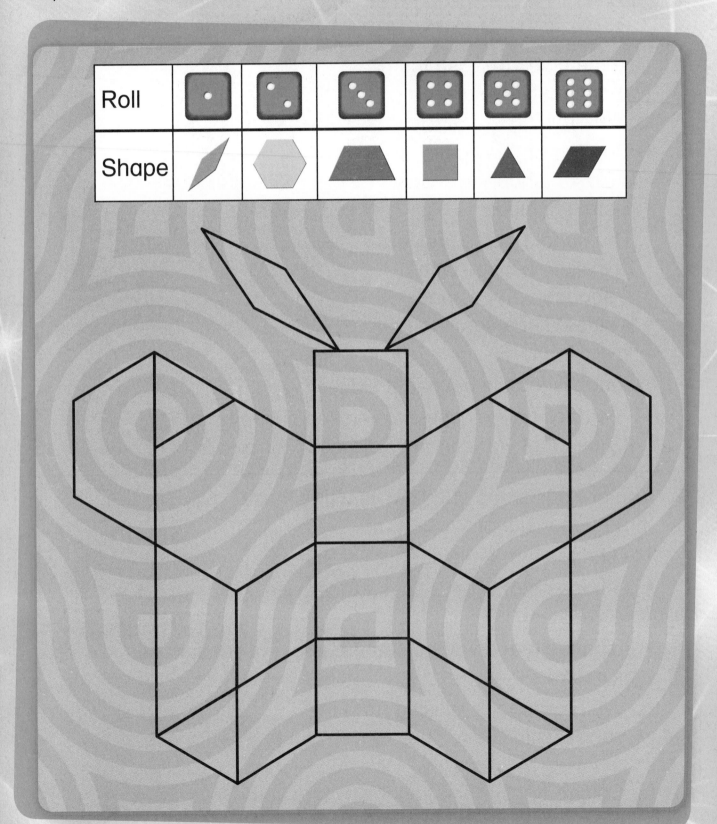

### 13.1 Sort Two-Dimensional Shapes

**1.** Circle the closed shapes with only 3 straight sides.

**2.**  **Structure** Draw 2 different two-dimensional shapes that have 1 or more L-shaped vertices.

### 13.2 Describe Two-Dimensional Shapes

Circle the attributes of the shape.

| 3. **Hexagon** | 4. **Rhombus** |
|---|---|
| 6 straight sides | 4 straight sides |
| 8 straight sides | 4 vertices |
| 8 vertices | 6 vertices |
| closed | open |

**5.** How many  make a ?

**6.** How many  make a ?

_____  make a .

_____  make a .

**13.4** **Create More Shapes**

**7.** Use  to make a □. Draw to show your work.

    **Step 1** →    **Step 2** →

**8.** Use  and □ to make a . Draw to show your work.

**Step 1** →    **Step 2** →

# 13.5 Take Apart Two-Dimensional Shapes

Draw two lines to show the parts.

**9.** 1 square and 2 triangles

**10.** 2 triangles and 1 square

# 13.6 Sort Three-Dimensional Shapes

**11.** Circle the shapes with flat surfaces that are all squares.

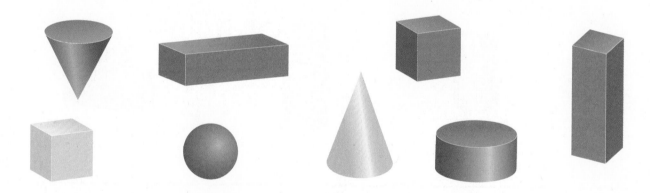

**12. Modeling Real Life** You need to find an object that has only flat surfaces for a scavenger hunt. Circle the objects you can use.

**13.7** **Describe Three-Dimensional Shapes**

Circle the attributes of the shape.

| **13.** **Rectangular Prism** | **14.** **Sphere** |
|---|---|
| 6 flat surfaces | 0 flat surfaces |
| 12 vertices | 1 flat surface |
| 12 edges | 0 edges |
| two-dimensional | rolls |

---

**13.8** **Combine Three-Dimensional Shapes**

**15.** Circle the new shape that you can make.

---

**13.9** **Take Apart Three-Dimensional Shapes**

**16.** Circle the shapes that make up the structure.

# 14

# Equal Shares

- ● What is your favorite food?
- ● How can you cut a sandwich so the pieces are the same size?

**Chapter Learning Target:**
Understand equal shares.

**Chapter Success Criteria:**
■ I can identify shapes that show equal shares.
■ I can explain which shapes are equal.
■ I can compare shares.
■ I can draw to show shares.

# Vocabulary

**Review Words**

bar graph
picture graph

## Organize It

Use the review words to complete the graphic organizer.

| Favorite Class | | | | | | | |
|---|---|---|---|---|---|---|---|
| Subject | | | | | | | |
| ✚ Math | | | | | | | |
| ♀ Science | | | | | | | |

0  1  2  3  4  5  6  7
**Number of students**

| Favorite Class | |
|---|---|
| ✚ Math | ☺ ☺ ☺ ☺ ☺ ☺ |
| ♀ Science | ☺ ☺ ☺ ☺ ☺ |

Each ☺ = 1 student.

## Define It

Use your vocabulary cards to complete the puzzle.

**Across**

1.

**Down**

2.
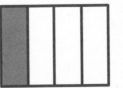

3.

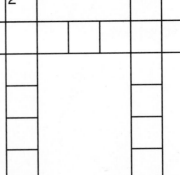

# Chapter 14 Vocabulary Cards

equal shares

fourth of

fourths

half of

halves

quarter of

quarters

unequal shares

A **fourth of** the rectangle is shaded.

The squares show **equal shares**.

**Half of** the circle is shaded.

The rectangle is divided into **fourths**.

A **quarter of** the rectangle is shaded.

This circle is divided into **halves**.

The shapes show **unequal shares**.

The rectangle is divided into **quarters**.

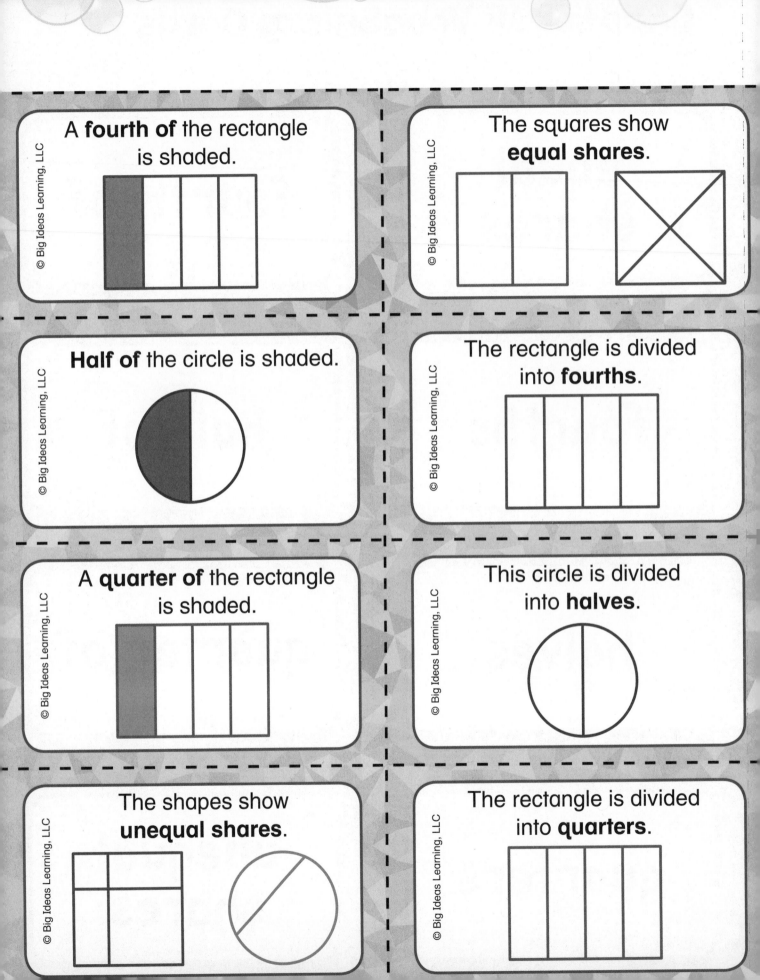

**Learning Target:** Identify equal shares in two-dimensional shapes.

Sort the Equal Shares Sort Cards.

| Equal Parts | Unequal Parts |
|---|---|
| | |

Circle the shape that shows equal shares.

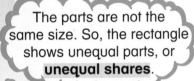

The parts are the same size. So, the rectangle shows equal parts, or **equal shares**.

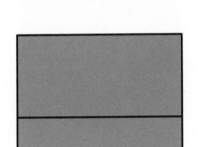

The parts are not the same size. So, the rectangle shows unequal parts, or **unequal shares**.

## Show and Grow

Circle the shape that shows equal shares.

**1.**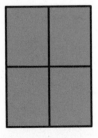

**2.**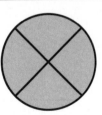

**3.**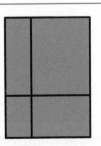

**4.**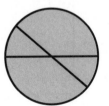

**Apply and Grow: Practice**

Circle the shape that shows equal shares.

**5.**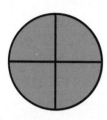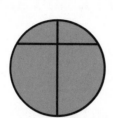

**6.**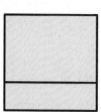

**7.**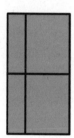

**8.**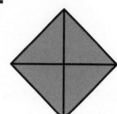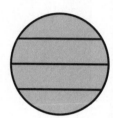

**9.**

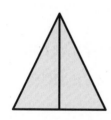

_____ equal shares

**10.**

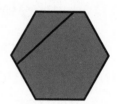

_____ equal shares

**11.** **YOU BE THE TEACHER** Newton says the shape shows equal shares. Is he correct? Explain.

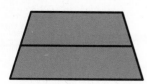 _____

_____

You and your friend each design a kite. Your kite has 2 equal shares. Your friend's has 2 unequal shares. Draw to show the parts.

You

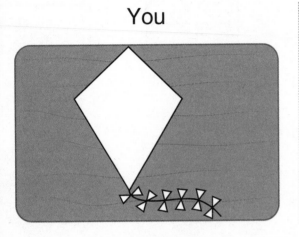

Friend

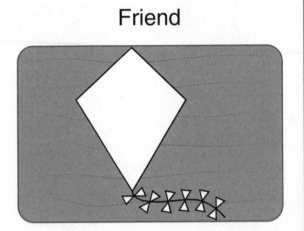

## Show and Grow

**12.** You and your friend each design a poster. Your poster has 4 unequal shares. Your friend's has 4 equal shares. Draw to show the parts.

You

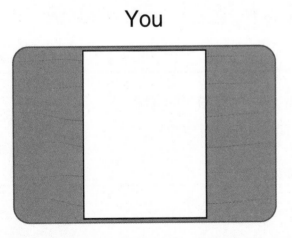

Friend

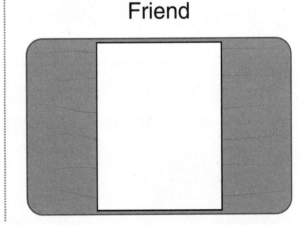

Name _____

**Learning Target:** Identify equal shares in two-dimensional shapes.

Equal Shares          Unequal Shares

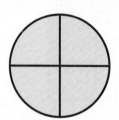     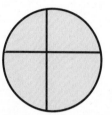     

Circle the shape that shows equal shares.

**1.**

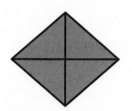     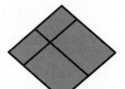

**2.**

     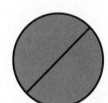

**3.**

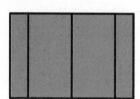     

**4.**

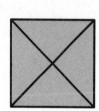     

**5.**

_____ equal shares

**6.**

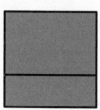

_____ equal shares

**7.** 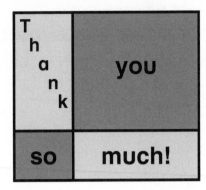 **Precision** Descartes makes a thank you card with 4 equal shares. Which card does Descartes make?

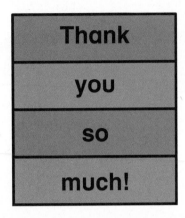

**8. Modeling Real Life** You and your friend each design a sticker. Your sticker has 2 unequal shares. Your friend's has 2 equal shares. Draw to show the parts.

You                                Friend

**Review & Refresh**

Make quick sketches to find the sum.

**9.**  32
      + 25

| Tens | Ones |
|------|------|
|      |      |
|      |      |

**10.**  61
       + 15

| Tens | Ones |
|------|------|
|      |      |
|      |      |

**Learning Target:** Identify shapes that show halves.

 Explore and Grow

Build hexagons with the pattern blocks shown.
Circle the hexagon that shows 2 equal shares.

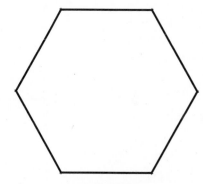

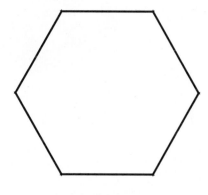

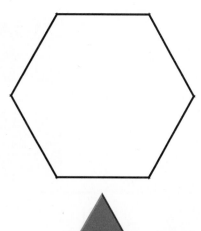

## Think and Grow

Circle the shape that shows halves.

This rectangle has 2 equal shares, or **halves**. Each equal share is **half of** the rectangle.

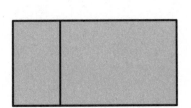

This rectangle does not have equal shares.

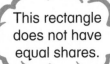

# Show and Grow

Circle the shape that shows halves.

1.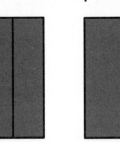

2.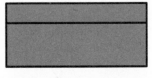

3.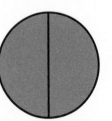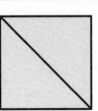

4.

## ✓ Apply and Grow: Practice

Circle the shapes that show halves.

**5.**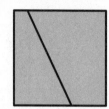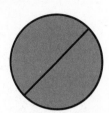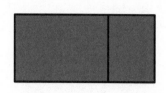

**6.**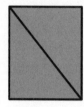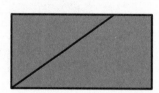

Color half of the shape.

**7.**     **8.** 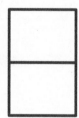    **9.**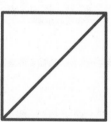

**10.** 🔷 **Structure** Match each half with its whole.

<u>Half</u>                    <u>Whole</u>

Show three ways to cut the cheese in half.

 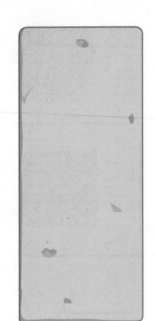 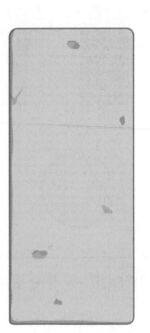

## Show and Grow

11. Show three ways to fold the rug in half.

Circle the shape that shows halves.

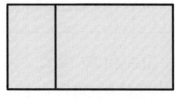

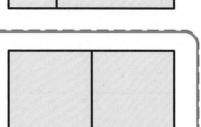

This rectangle has 2 equal shares, or **halves**. Each equal share is **half of** the rectangle.

Circle the shape that shows halves.

**1.**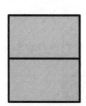

**2.**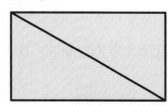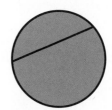

Circle the shapes that show halves.

**3.**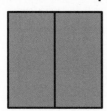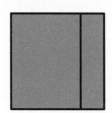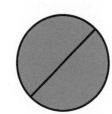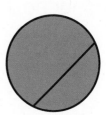

**4.**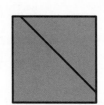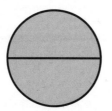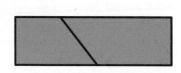

Color half of the shape.

**5.** 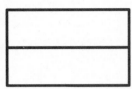  |  **6.** 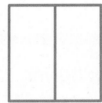  |  **7.**

---

**8.**  **YOU BE THE TEACHER** Newton says there are only two ways to divide a rectangle into halves. Is he correct? Explain.

_____

_____

---

**9. Modeling Real Life** Show three ways to fold the bandana in half.

**Review & Refresh**

**10.** Circle the shapes that only have a curved surface.

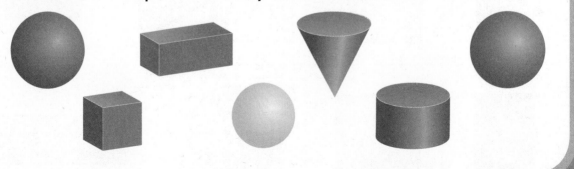

**Learning Target:** Identify shapes that show fourths.

 **Explore and Grow**

Sort the 2, 4, or Unequal Shares Sort Cards.

| 2 Equal Shares |
| --- |
|  |

| 4 Equal Shares |
| --- |
|  |

| Unequal Shares |
| --- |
|  |

This rectangle has 4 equal shares. The equal shares are called **fourths**, or **quarters**. Each equal share is a **fourth of**, or a **quarter of** the rectangle.

Circle the shape that shows fourths.

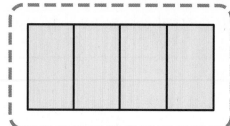

This rectangle does not have equal shares.

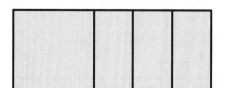

## Show and Grow

Circle the shape that shows fourths.

**1.**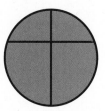

**2.**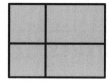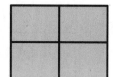

**3.**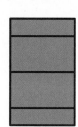

**4.**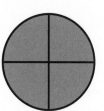

## ✓ Apply and Grow: Practice

Circle the shapes that show fourths.

**5.**

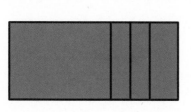
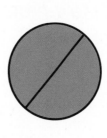
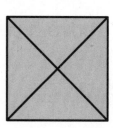

Color a quarter of the shape.

**6.**

**7.**

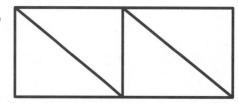

**8.** 🅜🅟 **Precision**  Draw more lines to show fourths.

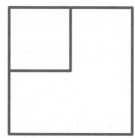

**9.** **DIG DEEPER!**  You cut a circle into halves. Your friend cuts the same-sized circle into quarters. Who has the larger pieces? Think: How do you know?

You                              Friend

You cut a pizza into quarters. Your friend eats I quarter. How many more friends could have a piece of pizza?

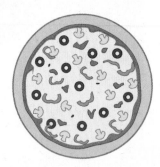

_____ friends

## Show and Grow

10. You cut a granola bar into quarters. Your friend eats 2 quarters. How many more friends could have a piece of the granola bar?

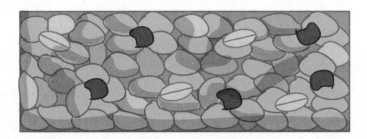

_____ friends

**Learning Target:** Identify shapes that show fourths.

### Circle the shape that shows fourths.

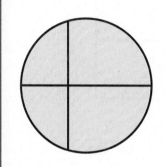 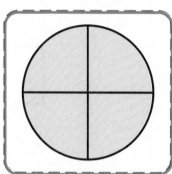

This circle has 4 equal shares. The equal shares are called fourths, or quarters.

### Circle the shape that shows fourths.

**1.**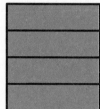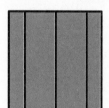

**2.**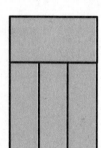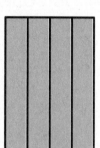

### Circle the shapes that show fourths.

**3.**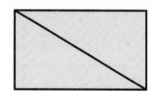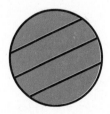

### Color a quarter of the shape.

**4.**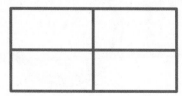

**5.**

**6.** **DIG DEEPER!** Which shape shows a fourth of a circle?

**7.** **MP Reasoning** Color half of the square. How many fourths did you color?

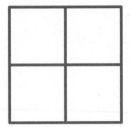

_____ fourths

**8.** **Modeling Real Life** You cut a slice of bread into quarters. Your friend eats 3 quarters. How many more friends could have a piece of bread?

_____ friend

**Review & Refresh**

Draw to show the time.

**9.**

**10.**

**1.** You, your friend, and your cousin are having a picnic. Use the clues to match each person with a food item.

- You bring an item that is cut into 4 unequal shares.
- Your friend brings an item that is cut into halves.
- Your cousin brings an item that is cut into quarters.

| You | Friend | Cousin |
|-----|--------|--------|

  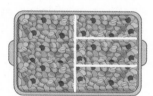

**2. a.** You cut an apple into 2 equal shares. You cut each share in half. How many equal shares do you have now?

_____ equal shares

Show how you know:

**b.** You give your friend a fourth of the apple. How many shares do you have left?

_____ shares

# Three In a Row: Equal Shares

**To Play:** Players take turns. On your turn, spin the spinner. Cover a square that matches your spin. Continue playing until a player gets three in a row.

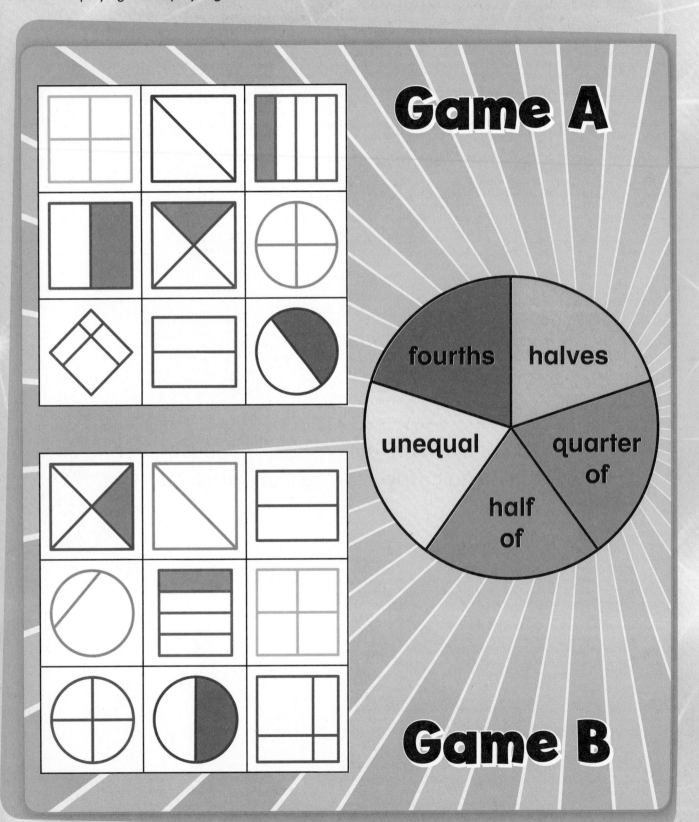

**Game A**

**Game B**

### 14.1 Equal Shares

1.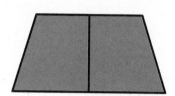

_____ equal shares

2.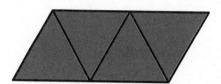

_____ equal shares

3. **Modeling Real Life** Newton and Descartes each design a place mat. Newton's has 4 equal shares. Descartes's has 4 unequal shares. Draw to show the parts.

Newton

Descartes

### 14.2 Partition Shapes into Halves

4. Circle the shapes that show halves.

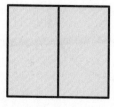
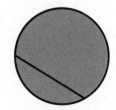
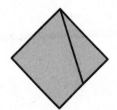
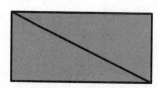

**5.** **MP** **Structure** Match each half with its whole.

Half         Whole

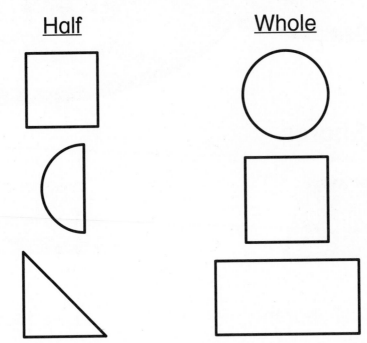

---

**14.3** **Partition Shapes into Fourths**

**6.** Circle the shapes that show fourths.

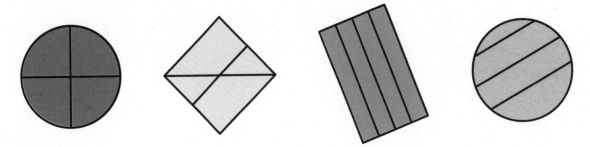

---

Color a quarter of the shape.

**7.**

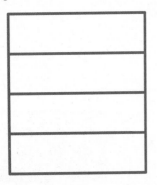

**8.**

**1.** Shade the circle next to the equation that tells how many fewer students chose manga comics than superhero comics.

| **Favorite Comics** | |
|---|---|
| Science Fiction | Ⅲ̶Ⅱ̶ |
| Superhero | Ⅲ̶Ⅱ̶ ||| |
| Manga | || |

○ $5 + 8 + 2 = 15$

○ $8 - 5 = 3$

○ $8 + 2 = 10$

○ $8 - 2 = 6$

---

**2.** Shade the circle next to the number that tells how many minutes are in a half hour.

○ 15      ○ 30      ○ 45      ○ 60

---

**3.** Shade the circle next to the shape that does *not* show fourths.

○

○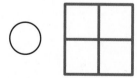

○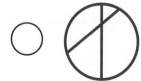

○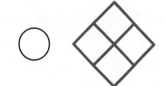

**4.** Shade the circle next to the shape that has no straight sides.

 ◯

◯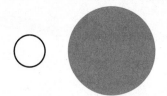

◯

◯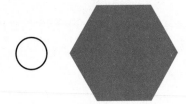

**5.** Shade the circle next to the difference.

$17 - 8 =$ _____

◯ 8     ◯ 9

◯ 10     ◯ 12

**6.** Draw lines to show halves.

**7.** Write the time on the clock two ways.

_____

_____ : _____

**8.**

cube

_____ flat surfaces

_____ vertices

_____ edges

---

**9.** Shade the circles next to the choices that match the model.

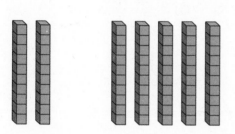

○ 7 ones

○ 2 tens + 5 tens

○ 70

○ 20 + 50

---

**10.** Shade the circles next to the choices that show the shapes you can use to make a .

© Big Ideas Learning, LLC

**11.** Tell how many equal shares.

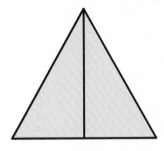

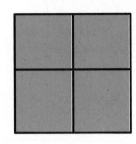

_____ equal shares          _____ equal shares

---

**12.** A group of students are at a park. 2 of them leave. There are 4 left. How many students were at the park to start?

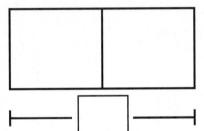

_____ – _____ = _____

_____ students

---

**13.** Circle the shapes that make up the structure.

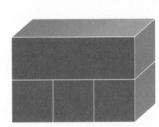

# Glossary

## A

### add   [sumar]

**2 + 4 = 6**

---

### addend   [sumando]

$$4 + 3 = 7$$

---

### addition equation
[ecuación de adición]

$$4 + 5 = 9$$

---

### analog clock   [reloj analogo]

## B

### bar graph   [gráfica de barras]

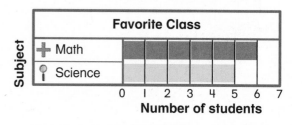

Favorite Class

Subject

Math
Science

Number of students

---

### bar model   [modelo de barra]

You: 5

Friend: 2 | 3

---

## C

### column   [columna]

| 1 | 2 | 3 | 4 | 5 | 6 | 7 | 8 | 9 | 10 |
|---|---|---|---|---|---|---|---|---|---|
| 11 | 12 | 13 | 14 | 15 | 16 | 17 | 18 | 19 | 20 |
| 21 | 22 | 23 | 24 | 25 | 26 | 27 | 28 | 29 | 30 |
| 31 | 32 | 33 | 34 | 35 | 36 | 37 | 38 | 39 | 40 |
| 41 | 42 | 43 | 44 | 45 | 46 | 47 | 48 | 49 | 50 |
| 51 | 52 | 53 | 54 | 55 | 56 | 57 | 58 | 59 | 60 |
| 61 | 62 | 63 | 64 | 65 | 66 | 67 | 68 | 69 | 70 |
| 71 | 72 | 73 | 74 | 75 | 76 | 77 | 78 | 79 | 80 |
| 81 | 82 | 83 | 84 | 85 | 86 | 87 | 88 | 89 | 90 |
| 91 | 92 | 93 | 94 | 95 | 96 | 97 | 98 | 99 | 100 |
| 101 | 102 | 103 | 104 | 105 | 106 | 107 | 108 | 109 | 110 |
| 111 | 112 | 113 | 114 | 115 | 116 | 117 | 118 | 119 | 120 |

**compare**   [comparar]

There are more red cubes than yellow cubes.

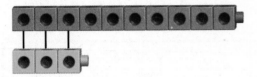

**count back**   [contar hacia atrás]

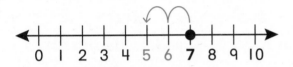

**count on**   [contar]

**curved surface**   [superficie curva]

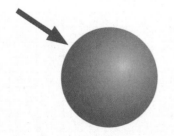

**data**   [datos]

Favorite Class

| math | science |
| science | math |
| science | math |
| math | science |
| math | science |
| math | |

**decade numbers**
[números de la década]

| 1 | 2 | 3 | 4 | 5 | 6 | 7 | 8 | 9 | 10 |
|---|---|---|---|---|---|---|---|---|---|
| 11 | 12 | 13 | 14 | 15 | 16 | 17 | 18 | 19 | 20 |
| 21 | 22 | 23 | 24 | 25 | 26 | 27 | 28 | 29 | 30 |
| 31 | 32 | 33 | 34 | 35 | 36 | 37 | 38 | 39 | 40 |
| 41 | 42 | 43 | 44 | 45 | 46 | 47 | 48 | 49 | 50 |
| 51 | 52 | 53 | 54 | 55 | 56 | 57 | 58 | 59 | 60 |
| 61 | 62 | 63 | 64 | 65 | 66 | 67 | 68 | 69 | 70 |
| 71 | 72 | 73 | 74 | 75 | 76 | 77 | 78 | 79 | 80 |
| 81 | 82 | 83 | 84 | 85 | 86 | 87 | 88 | 89 | 90 |
| 91 | 92 | 93 | 94 | 95 | 96 | 97 | 98 | 99 | 100 |
| 101 | 102 | 103 | 104 | 105 | 106 | 107 | 108 | 109 | 110 |
| 111 | 112 | 113 | 114 | 115 | 116 | 117 | 118 | 119 | 120 |

**difference**   [diferencia]

$$8 - 3 = 5$$

**digit**   [dígito]

The digits of 16 are 1 and 6.

16

**digital clock**  [reloj digital]

**doubles**  [dobles]

$$4 + 4 = 8$$

**doubles minus 1**
[dobles menos 1]

$$4 + 4 = 8, \text{ so } 4 + 3 = 7$$

**doubles plus 1**
[dobles más 1]

$$4 + 4 = 8, \text{ so } 4 + 5 = 9$$

**E**

**edge**  [arista]

**equal shares**  [partes iguales]

The squares show
**equal shares**.

 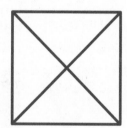

**equals**  [igual]

$$8 + 2 = 10$$

8 plus 2 equals 10

**fact family**   [hecho de la familia]

$$2 + 3 = 5$$
$$3 + 2 = 5$$
$$5 - 2 = 3$$
$$5 - 3 = 2$$

**fewer**   [menos]

**flat surface**   [superficie plana]

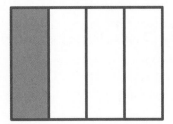

**fourth of**   [cuarto de]

A **fourth of** the rectangle
is shaded.

**fourths**   [cuartos]

The rectangle is divided
into **fourths**.

**greater than**   [mayor que]

26 is greater than 23.

26 > 23

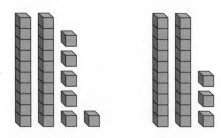

**half hour**   [media hora]

A half hour is 30 minutes.

**half of**   [mitad de]

**Half of** the circle is shaded.

**half past**   [y media]

half past 3

**halves**   [mitades]

This circle is divided
into **halves**.

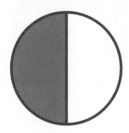

**hour**   [hora]

An hour is 60 minutes.

**hour hand**   [horario]

L

**length**   [longitud]

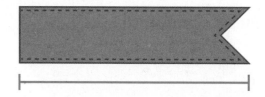

**length unit**   [unidad de longitud]

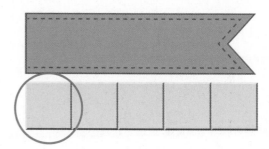

**less than**  [menor que]

22 is less than 38.

22 < 38

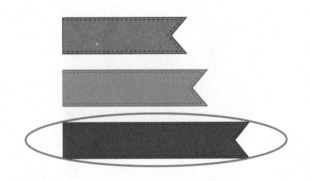

**longest**  [más largo]

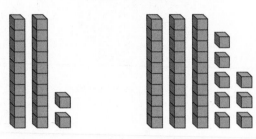

**M**

**measure**  [medida]

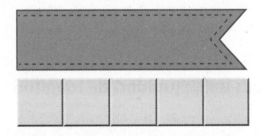

**minus**  [menos]

# 3 − 1
## 3 minus 1

**minute**  [minuto]

60 minutes is 1 hour.

**minute hand**  [minutero]

**more**  [más]

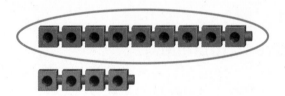

**N**

**number line**  [numero de linea]

## O

**o'clock**   [en punto]

3 o'clock

**120 chart**   [120 gráfico]

| 1 | 2 | 3 | 4 | 5 | 6 | 7 | 8 | 9 | 10 |
|---|---|---|---|---|---|---|---|---|---|
| 11 | 12 | 13 | 14 | 15 | 16 | 17 | 18 | 19 | 20 |
| 21 | 22 | 23 | 24 | 25 | 26 | 27 | 28 | 29 | 30 |
| 31 | 32 | 33 | 34 | 35 | 36 | 37 | 38 | 39 | 40 |
| 41 | 42 | 43 | 44 | 45 | 46 | 47 | 48 | 49 | 50 |
| 51 | 52 | 53 | 54 | 55 | 56 | 57 | 58 | 59 | 60 |
| 61 | 62 | 63 | 64 | 65 | 66 | 67 | 68 | 69 | 70 |
| 71 | 72 | 73 | 74 | 75 | 76 | 77 | 78 | 79 | 80 |
| 81 | 82 | 83 | 84 | 85 | 86 | 87 | 88 | 89 | 90 |
| 91 | 92 | 93 | 94 | 95 | 96 | 97 | 98 | 99 | 100 |
| 101 | 102 | 103 | 104 | 105 | 106 | 107 | 108 | 109 | 110 |
| 111 | 112 | 113 | 114 | 115 | 116 | 117 | 118 | 119 | 120 |

**ones**   [unidades]

23 has 3 ones.

**ones place**   [un lugar]

2<u>3</u>

**open number line**
[abrir la línea numérica]

## P

**part**   [parte]

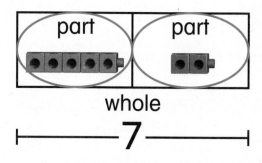

whole
7

**part-part-whole model**
[modelo parte-parte-todo]

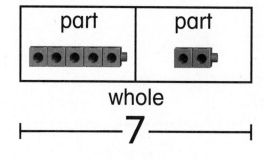

whole
7

**picture graph**   [gráfico de imagen]

| Favorite Class | | | | | | |
|---|---|---|---|---|---|---|
| ➕ Math | ☺ | ☺ | ☺ | ☺ | ☺ | ☺ |
| 👤 Science | ☺ | ☺ | ☺ | ☺ | ☺ | |

Each ☺ = 1 student.

**plus** [más]

$$2 + 1$$

2 plus 1

**quarter of** [cuarta parte de]

A **quarter of** the rectangle is shaded.

**quarters** [cuartas partes]

The rectangle is divided into **quarters**.

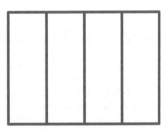

**rectangular prism** [prisma rectangular]

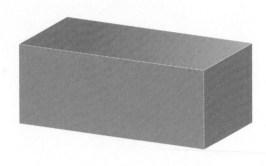

**rhombus** [rombo]

**row** [fila]

| 1 | 2 | 3 | 4 | 5 | 6 | 7 | 8 | 9 | 10 |
|---|---|---|---|---|---|---|---|---|---|
| 11 | 12 | 13 | 14 | 15 | 16 | 17 | 18 | 19 | 20 |
| 21 | 22 | 23 | 24 | 25 | 26 | 27 | 28 | 29 | 30 |
| 31 | 32 | 33 | 34 | 35 | 36 | 37 | 38 | 39 | 40 |
| 41 | 42 | 43 | 44 | 45 | 46 | 47 | 48 | 49 | 50 |
| 51 | 52 | 53 | 54 | 55 | 56 | 57 | 58 | 59 | 60 |
| 61 | 62 | 63 | 64 | 65 | 66 | 67 | 68 | 69 | 70 |
| 71 | 72 | 73 | 74 | 75 | 76 | 77 | 78 | 79 | 80 |
| 81 | 82 | 83 | 84 | 85 | 86 | 87 | 88 | 89 | 90 |
| 91 | 92 | 93 | 94 | 95 | 96 | 97 | 98 | 99 | 100 |
| 101 | 102 | 103 | 104 | 105 | 106 | 107 | 108 | 109 | 110 |
| 111 | 112 | 113 | 114 | 115 | 116 | 117 | 118 | 119 | 120 |

# S

**shortest**  [el más corto]

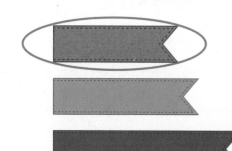

**side**  [lado]

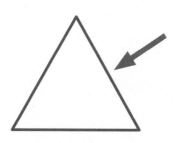

**subtract**  [restar]

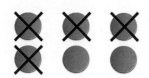

$$6 - 4 = 2$$

**subtraction equation**
[ecuación de resta]

$$9 - 5 = 4$$

**sum**  [suma]

$$5 + 3 = 8$$

# T

**tally chart**  [tabla de conteo]

| Favorite Class | |
|---|---|
| ➕ Math | ⵑⵑⵑ I |
| 🔍 Science | ⵑⵑⵑ |

**tally mark**  [marca de conteo]

| Favorite Class | |
|---|---|
| ➕ Math | ⵑⵑⵑ① |
| 🔍 Science | ⵑⵑⵑ |

$$| = 1, \; ⵑⵑⵑ = 5$$

**tens**  [decenas]

23 has 2 tens.

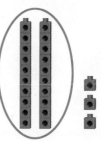

**tens place**  [lugar de decenas]

2<u>3</u>

---

**three-dimensional shape**
[forma tridimensional]

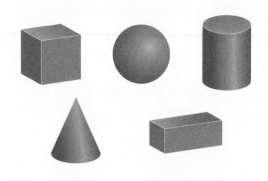

---

**trapezoid**  [trapecio]

---

**two-dimensional shape**
[forma bidimensional]

---

 **U**

**unequal shares**
[partes desiguales]

The shapes show
**unequal shares**.

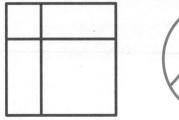

---

 **V**

**vertex**  [vértice]

---

 **W**

**whole**  [todo]

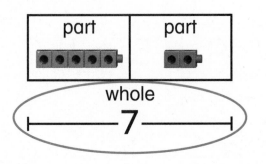

# Index

telling time to
> hour and minute hands for, 595–600
>
> hour hand for, 589–594

**Half past**
> on analog and digital clocks, 601–606
>
> definition of, 590
>
> hour and minute hands showing, 595–600
>
> hour hand showing, 589–594

**Halves**
> definition of, 682
>
> identifying shapes showing, 681–686

**Hexagons**
> combining, to make new shapes, 628, 631
>
> combining shapes to make, 626–629
>
> definition of, 620
>
> describing, 619–624
>
> equal shares in, identifying, 677, 681
>
> halves of, 681
>
> taking apart, 639, 642

**Higher Order Thinking,** *See* Dig Deeper

**Hour**
> on analog and digital clocks, 601–606
>
> definition of, 584
>
> telling time to
>> hour and minute hands for, 595–600
>>
>> hour hand for, 583–588

**Hour hand**
> definition of, 584
>
> using to tell time to half hour, 589–594
>
> using to tell time to hour, 583–588
>
> using to tell time to hour and half hour, 595–600

**Hundred chart**
> for adding 10, 404, 406
>
> for adding tens and ones, 465–470
>
> for subtracting 10, 410, 413

**L**

**Learning Target,** *In every lesson. For example, see:* 3, 65, 127, 187, 243, 293, 355, 459, 503, 541

**Length**
> comparing indirectly, 509–514
>
> measuring
>> using color tiles, 516–526
>>
>> using like objects, 515–520
>>
>> using paper clips, 521–526
>
> ordering objects by, 503–508
>
> solving compare problems involving, 527–532

**Length unit**
> color tiles of, 516–520
>
> definition of, 516

**Less than (<),** 356, 373–378 (*See also* Comparing numbers)

**Linking cubes**
> for add to problems, 3, 9, 10, 13
>
> for adding 0, 65
>
> for adding 1, 77
>
> for adding doubles, 84–88, 90, 188, 189, 191
>
> for adding in any order, 96, 97, 99
>
> for adding three numbers, 205
>
> for adding within 20, 233
>
> for completing fact families, 169
>
> for composing numbers
>> 11 to 19, 306, 309
>>
>> decade numbers (tens), 312–316
>
> for doubles minus 1 strategy, 90, 91, 93, 194, 195, 197
>
> for doubles plus 1 strategy, 90, 91, 93, 194, 195, 197
>
> for grouping by 10, 312–316
>
> for put together problems, 21
>
> for take from problems, 27, 28, 31

**Logic,** 67, 70, 473, 476

**Longest**
> definition of, 504
>
> ordering objects by, 503–508

**L-shaped vertices,** 615, 616, 619, 622

**Q**

**Quick sketches**

for adding tens to number, 446, 449

for comparing numbers, 357, 359, 365, 373–375, 444

for modeling numbers as tens and ones, 323–328, 360

for modeling two-digit numbers, 329–334

## R

**Reading,** *Throughout. For example, see:* T-7, T-87, T-155, T-247, T-297, T-425, T-513, T-551, T-587, T-679

**Real World,** *See* Modeling Real Life

**Reasoning,** *Throughout. For example, see:* 122, 153, 189, 461, 520, 543, 624, 639, 642, 692

**Rectangles**

combining, to make squares, 632

combining shapes to make, 626, 627, 633

definition of, 620

describing, 619–624

equal shares in, identifying, 676, 677, 679, 680

fourths, 688–692

halves, 682–686

as flat surfaces, of shapes, 644–648

taking apart shapes containing, 637–642

**Rectangular prisms**

combining, to make new shapes, 655–657, 659

definition of, 650

describing, 649–654

taking apart shapes containing, 661–666

**Repeated Reasoning,** 135

**Response to Intervention,** *Throughout. For example, see:* T-1B, T-115, T-137, T-201, T-241B, T-333, T-443, T-539B, T-587, T-615

**Review & Refresh,** *In every lesson. For example, see:* 8, 76, 210, 278, 372, 444, 514, 588, 624, 692

**Rhombus**

combining shapes to make, 627, 628, 633, 635

definition of, 620

describing, 619–624

**Rows**

in 120 chart, 293–294

in hundred chart, 404, 406, 410, 413

## S

**Scaffolding Instruction,** *In every lesson. For example, see:* T-5, T-147, T-231, T-337, T-369, T-411, T-505, T-555, T-645, T-689

**Shapes,** *See also specific shapes*

three-dimensional

combining to make new shapes, 655–660

curved surfaces of, 644–648

describing, 649–654

edges of, 650–654

flat surfaces of, 644–654

sorting, 643–648

taking apart, 661–666

vertices of, 649–654

two-dimensional

closed or open, 614–618

combining to make new shapes, 625–636

definition of, 614

describing, 619–624

equal shares in, fourths, 687–692

equal shares in, halves, 681–686

equal shares in, identifying, 675–680

number of sides, 614–624

number of vertices, 614–624

sorting, 613–618

taking apart, 637–642

**Shortest**

definition of, 504

ordering objects by, 503–508

**Show and Grow,** *In every lesson. For example, see:* 4, 66, 128, 188, 244, 294, 356, 404, 460, 504

**Show how you know,** *Throughout. For example, see:* 24, 295, 208, 235, 278, 301, 349, 588

**Sides, of two-dimensional shapes**
definition of, 614
describing, 619–624
sorting by number of, 614–618

**Smaller unknown, compare problems with,** 151–156

**Spheres**
combining with other shapes, 655
definition of, 650
describing, 649–654
taking apart shapes containing, 661

**Squares**
combining, to make new shapes, 627, 635
combining shapes to make, 632
definition of, 620
describing, 619–624
equal shares in, identifying, 676, 677, 679, 680
 fourths, 688, 689, 691, 692
 halves, 682, 683, 685, 686
as flat surfaces, of shapes, 644–648
taking apart shapes containing, 637–642

**Start, unknown**
add to problems with, 127–132
take from problems with, 139–144

**Straight sides, of two-dimensional shapes**
describing, 619–624
number of, 614–618

**Structure,** *Throughout. For example, see:* 47, 50, 53, 73, 109, 129, 141, 171, 201, 260, 295, 384, 423, 467, 683

**Subtraction**
of 0 or all, 71–76
of 1, 77–82

using addition to subtract strategy, 113–118
 within 20, 249–254
 of tens, 439–444
using bar model, within 20, 281, 282
using "count back" strategy, 107–112, 434, 437
 within 20, 243–248, 280
using "count on" strategy, 250–254, 440, 443
definition of, 28
using "get to 10" strategy, 261–266, 426
 subtracting 9 in, 255–260
solving problems using
 within 20, 279–284
 how many fewer, 39–44, 151–156
 how many more, 34–38
 smaller unknown, 151–156
 take apart, connected with put together, 51–56
 take from, 27–32
 take from, with change unknown, 133–138
 take from, with start unknown, 139–144
of tens, 427–432
 using addition to subtract strategy, 439–444
 using mental math, 409–414
 on number line, 433–438

**Subtraction equations,** *See also* Subtraction
completing fact families with, 169–174, 520
how many fewer, 40–44
how many more, 34–38
take apart, 52–56
take from, 27–32
true or false, 157–162, 267–272, 372, 482
writing, 28–32

**Success Criteria,** *In every lesson. For example, see:* T-3, T-71, T-139, T-267, T-323, T-445, T-521, T-583, T-661, T-687

**Unknown start**
    add to problems with, 127–132
    take from problems with, 139–144

**Vertex (vertices)**
    definition of, 614
    of three-dimensional shapes, 649–654
    of two-dimensional shapes
        describing, 619–624
        L-shaped, 615, 616, 619, 622
        sorting by number of, 614–618

**Which One Doesn't Belong?,** 603, 606
**Whole,** *See also* Part–part–whole model
    definition of, 16
    equal shares in
        fourths, 687–692
        halves, 681–686
        identifying, 675–680
    put together problems for finding, 15–20
    subtraction equation for finding, 139–144
**Word problems, solving**
    with addition, 489–494
        within 20, 229–234
        add to, 3–14
        add to, with missing addend, 45–50
        bigger unknown, 145–150
        put together, 15–20
        put together, connected with take
            apart, 51–56

        put together, missing both addends,
            21–26
    with subtraction
        within 20, 279–284
        how many fewer, 39–44
        how many more, 33–38
        smaller unknown, 151–156
        take apart, connected with put
            together, 51–56
        take from, 27–32
**Writing,** 549, 552
**Writing equations**
    addition, 3–8
    subtraction, 28–32
**Writing numbers**
    11 to 19, 305–310
    to 120, 341–346
    counting by tens and ones for, 317–322
    decade numbers (tens), 311–316
    in different ways, 335–340
    quick sketches for, 323–328, 360
    understanding place value in, 329–334

**You Be the Teacher,** *Throughout. For example,*
    *see:* 79, 115, 231, 275, 301, 411,
    479, 505, 597, 677

**Zero (0)**
    adding, 65–70
    subtracting, 71–76

# Reference Sheet

## Symbols

| | |
|---|---|
| + | plus |
| − | minus |
| = | equals |
| > | greater than |
| < | less than |

## Doubles

| | |
|---|---|
| $1 + 1 = 2$ | $6 + 6 = 12$ |
| $2 + 2 = 4$ | $7 + 7 = 14$ |
| $3 + 3 = 6$ | $8 + 8 = 16$ |
| $4 + 4 = 8$ | $9 + 9 = 18$ |
| $5 + 5 = 10$ | $10 + 10 = 20$ |

## Equal Shares

fourths
quarters

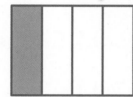

fourth of
quarter of

halves

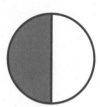

half of

## Time

analog clock

digital clock

An hour is
60 minutes.

A half hour
is 30 minutes.

minute
hand

hour
hand

4 o'clock

half past 4

# Two-Dimensional Shapes

 **triangle** — 3 straight sides, 3 vertices

 **rectangle** — 4 straight sides, 4 vertices

 **square** — 4 straight sides, 4 vertices

 **hexagon** — 6 straight sides, 6 vertices

 **trapezoid** — 4 straight sides, 4 vertices

 **rhombus** — 4 straight sides, 4 vertices

# Three-Dimensional Shapes

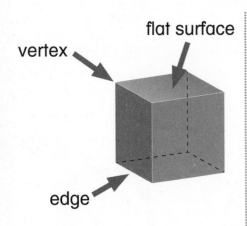

vertex

flat surface

edge

 **cube** — 6 flat surfaces, 8 vertices, 12 edges

 **rectangular prism** — 6 flat surfaces, 8 vertices, 12 edges

 **cone** — 1 flat surface, 1 vertex, 0 edges

 **cylinder** — 2 flat surfaces, 0 vertices, 0 edges

**sphere** — 0 flat surfaces, 0 vertices, 0 edges

# Credits